Thread Painting
with Style

Nancy Prince

Located in Paducah, Kentucky, the American Quilter's Society (AQS) is dedicated to promoting the accomplishments of today's quilters. Through its publications and events, AQS strives to honor today's quiltmakers and their work and to inspire future creativity and innovation in quiltmaking.

Executive Book Editor: Andi Milam Reynolds
Copy Editor: Chrystal Abhalter
Graphic Design: Joyce Robinson
Cover Design: Michael Buckingham
Photography: Charles R. Lynch

Additional copies of this book may be ordered from the American Quilter's Society, PO Box 3290, Paducah, KY 42002-3290, or online at www.AmericanQuilter.com.

Text © 2011, Author, Nancy Prince
Artwork © 2011, American Quilter's Society

Library of Congress Cataloging-in-Publication Data

Prince, Nancy (Nancy J.)
  Thread painting with style / by Nancy Prince.
    p. cm.
  ISBN 978-1-57432-646-8
  1. Embroidery, Machine--Patterns. I. Title.
TT772.P75 2011
746.44'041--dc23
                                            2011017238

Title page:
SEARCHING FOR BUTTERFLIES, *detail.*
Full quilt on page 108.

Right:
LIFE IN HOLLY RIDGE, *detail. Full quilt on pages 6–7.*

Dedication

To my wonderful and talented family.

They each possess an assortment of wonderful blessings and gifts and make every day worthwhile and all things possible.

Table of Contents

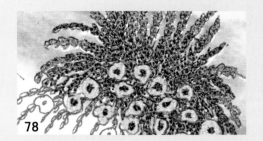

Introduction

Thread painting is a fun and exciting way to add pizzazz to a quilt by using fabric or stabilizer as your canvas and thread as your medium. Think of the sewing machine needle as the paintbrush or colored pencil and the thread as your paint or color. To create the design, simply move the hoop. This allows the needle to paint (or color) each thread where it needs to go. A straight or zigzag stitch does all the work, so no specific sewing machine is required.

One of the most common remarks I hear from students is that thread painting looks hard. Yes, some designs do look difficult, but remember that looks can be deceiving. Thread painting is actually very simple—just take it one step at a time. I have explained the process step-by-step and it is most definitely doable. Thread painting is as easy as painting by number or coloring in a coloring book.

Many students assume they have to be a trained or talented artist to be successful. Not so! Painting and drawing are enviable talents to possess but talents I unfortunately don't have (you may feel this way yourself). Success for me was finding a way around this apparent obstacle. I hope this book will demonstrate that drawing and painting skills are not mandatory and you can be successful right from the start. If you are the consummate artist, then I hope the information and projects in this book will help further your artistic skills.

One of the reasons thread painted designs appear difficult is because they look realistic. This realism is achieved by successfully shading, blending, and highlighting the design so the final product appears as it does in nature. After you read about thread, supplies, stitches, and methods, the four circle quilts are a simple way to learn to shade, blend, and highlight, and to grasp the basics of thread painting. *SEARCHING FOR BUTTERFLIES* is the next natural step to improve your shading and blending techniques. Thread sketching is introduced in *POPPIES ON PARADE* as a way to use thread as the design element and to show how it can be used to augment commercial fabric or to enhance your own custom printed fabric.

One of the perks of buying a quilt book when contemplating a new technique is that the person writing the book has made the mistakes, worked them out, and presents information to you to make the process easier. I learned early on that each quilt I made presented new challenges and problems and gave me the chance to perfect what I had learned so far. Just when I thought I had mastered a technique, something else would rear its head. I finally realized that my thread painting adventure would be constantly evolving, and I am hopeful there will always be new challenges to address. For me, that is certainly an exciting scenario. I hope it will be for you, too.

LIFE IN HOLLY RIDGE, *75" x 54", made by the author*

An Adventure in
Thread Painting

Thread Painting with Style NANCY PRINCE

LONGING FOR THE PAST, *51" x 31",
made by the author*

Quilts have become an integral part of most of our lives, and whether the intended use is for competition or to snuggle underneath on a cold winter night, each quilt has a specific use or a story to tell. Most quilts have a good dose of inspiration, a little or a lot of creativity, and some a uniqueness that sets them apart from every other quilt. But they all are a part of our lives and that is what makes them special to each of us.

Landscapes and nature are a huge part of my quilting world. I find that making landscape quilts gives me a sense of freedom. It allows me to create something in fabric and thread that has some meaning for me; I can capture a snapshot of time in each quilt I make. Thread early on became the center of my quilting adventure.

Confusion was an understatement as I stood in front of row upon row of thread racks, each tempting me with their luscious and inviting colors and begging for a good home. The only problem—I was totally intimidated because I didn't know where to start and what to buy. Through the years I have educated myself about which threads to use. Hopefully, the information I've compiled here will answer some of your questions so you can experience some of the exciting thread painting paths I have followed.

It seems like every day there is a new version of an old thread or a completely new thread enticing our buying power. Thread manufacturers are always one step ahead of us. They anticipate our needs many times before we even know a need exists. Sometimes our ideas as quilters, seamstresses, or embroiderers push the envelope, creating a new thread need that thread manufacturers are only too happy to help us with.

The quilting world is also constantly changing and growing, and every magazine and book is stocked with fresh and exciting ways to make old ideas new. In this process, new products emerge. These new products equal exciting new projects that cause our creative urges to soar constantly, again pushing the envelope even further. It is a beautiful circle in which one idea spurs on another one.

The best part of my thread adventure came one day when I realized that I, as a quilter, am part of a large and ever-growing community of women and men all embarking on the same path—how to spice up their next quilt to create something different and exciting. It is my hope that this book will trigger some new ideas and help you forge ahead with your own designs in thread to create something unique and meaningful in your next quilt. So let's start where all this began—with the thread.

THREAD WEIGHT

It was so much simpler in the old days when we basically only had one thread choice. The selection was either cotton or cotton. Now we have a zillion manufacturers, colors, types, and weights of thread—the list is endless (see photo above). As a quilter and thread painter, I want to use them all, but I also want to be able to choose wisely based on the project at hand. Productivity at the sewing machine is in direct correlation to good organization, and, most importantly, being educated on which thread to select for which job.

Getting to Know *Thread*

One way threads are categorized is by weight. This weight provides a road map to determine which thread to choose.

When purchasing thread, the higher the thread weight or number, the thinner the thread. For example, a 60-weight thread is thinner than a 30-weight thread, but note that all threads of a given weight aren't created equal. Trust your eyes and fingers more than the number to get the result you want.

Normally the thread weight is shown on either the side of the bottom rim or on the bottom of the spool as a number, such as 40. Some are predominately displayed, others you have to work to find, and some aren't there at all.

POLYESTER

Polyester threads have delicious colors, emit a beautiful sheen, and give a bit of spark to the completed design, plus they stitch in smoothly and evenly. Their popularity with quilters, seamstresses, and embroiderers makes them readily available. Polyester threads are a dream to thread paint with because they have little breakage or shredding problems. Use weights 30, 35, 40, 60, and 100 for thread painting.

30- and 35-weight

These heavier weight threads, mostly the solid variety, work great when the design to thread paint needs a strong visual impact. These threads fill in faster than a 40-weight thread and stand out in a crowd, so don't use them in small confining areas.

Variegated or twist threads are available and work best for trunk or tree canopies, fences, or for designs where the thread

needs to stand out more or a bolder look is required. If you are looking for a 35-weight variegated thread, try YLI's Variations™ line.

40-weight

Forty-weight polyester thread is the most versatile thread weight for me because it is heavy enough to fill in quickly, but not so heavy that it can't be controlled in relatively small areas. Plus, the selection of colors and manufacturers is huge. Forty-weight threads are available in solid and variegated colors. For maximum performance they work best in small, uncluttered areas or large wide-open designs.

Solid 40-weight thread (or any solid thread for that matter) works best for blending, shading, and highlighting because you can control exactly where you want individual colors to go. Appropriate uses for solid color threads would be peoples' clothing, skin and hair; animals; birds; inanimate objects; tree trunks and canopies; and most landscape vegetation.

Most variegated polyester threads are either 35- or 40-weight. Variegated threads minimize the number of thread changes but do not work particularly well when blending and shading because the constantly changing thread color makes it difficult to control where individual colors land. Variegated threads can vary from soft, subtle light-to-dark color changes in the same color family to dramatic, bold color changes such as purple-to red-to-gold-to-yellow.

Brands vary, too. Variegated color runs can range from short 1" runs to over 4". The short runs are easier for me to manipulate, so I look for Superior, Mettler®,

*Figure 2-1
A variety of
threads*

*Figure 2-2
Dog's teeth detail
from Life in Holly
Ridge, pages 6-7*

60-weight bobbin

In the bobbin, use a 60-weight bobbin fill, lingerie, or embroidery thread. The fineness helps keep excessive thread from building up on the back of the design. All bobbin thread is not created equal, so choose carefully. I prefer Bottom Line by Superior Threads. It is a polyester thread so it leaves no lint in the bobbin case and it stitches out beautifully.

Choose a medium to light gray for most designs. The exception is to use white bobbin thread for white or pastel top threads because gray will shadow through, causing a white thread to appear gray. Try using a black thread under dark upper threads if thread tension is an issue.

Invisible

Anytime someone mentions invisible thread, some students automatically think of the old nylon thread we all loved to hate. Today's polyester invisible thread is a totally different story. Superior's MonoPoly doesn't break, won't turn yellow or brittle, and quilts in very softly. Invisible thread as it relates to thread painting is used to stitch the thread appliqués to the quilt top, underlay complex or busy designs, and for quilting the quilt top.

and Isacord® threads in 40-weight. Best uses for variegated threads would be tree trunks and canopies; distant flowers and vegetation; and small, up-close, multicolored flowers.

60- and 100-weight

These fine threads, almost exclusively sold in solid colors, work well when thread needs to blend in within confined areas or when the design area to thread paint is very small. The thinness of the thread allows time for the needle to stitch in small amounts of thread in very small areas, keeping the detail accurate. The thinness also allows room for more thread color changes in small confined areas, giving the design more depth and realism. Also, subtle highlighting and shading can be added over the final thread work to add more realism. As a comparison, a 40-weight thread in the same small confined area would fill in too quickly, resulting in blobs of thread in a small area rather than specific detail. Use a size 60 Microtex sharp needle with these thread weights.

● RAYON

Rayon thread, which stitches in a bit softer than polyester, is not as available. Some are not guaranteed to be colorfast, so be careful when using them on clothing if bleaching might be a concern. The normal thread painting weight for rayon is 30, 35, or 40. Sulky makes beautiful solid and variegated 40-weight threads. Just be aware that the color runs are fairly long in variegated versions.

COTTON

Most quilters and seamstresses prefer 50-weight cotton for piecing and general sewing. Cotton is a natural fiber; once thread painted in place, it produces a flat appearance. From my perspective, the flat appearance of the thread prohibits its wide use in thread painting, plus the stencil cutter tends to singe the edge of the design rather than fuse when removing the tulle in the Tulle Sandwich method (see page 39).

50- AND 100-WEIGHT SILK AND METALLIC

These very fine solid threads used sparingly have their place in thread painting. Both 50- and 100-weight threads are so thin that even the smallest detail can be thread painted with success (use a size 60 Microtex sharp needle). The thread virtually sinks into the fabric or stabilizer, allowing time to thread paint intricate areas to perfection. For example, the dog's teeth and gums in Figure 2-2 were only $\frac{1}{8}$" wide and $\frac{1}{16}$" high. The thinness of 100-weight silk thread gave the detail necessary for a realistic design. Both Superior Threads and YLI make beautiful silk threads.

If you are looking for a 100-weight variegated or metallic thread, YLI can fill the bill. Thread painting or quilting with a 100-weight variegated or metallic thread is like stitching onto a cloud. The transition from color to color in the variegated thread is almost unnoticeable and the sparkle from the metallic is breathtaking. Thread painting with these threads is effortless and they are a dream to quilt with.

Thread color tips

– – – Choose a thread at least 2 shades darker than what you think you need, as thread stitches in lighter than the color you see on the spool.

– – – Changing the direction of the thread within the design can slightly change the color of the thread. Light hitting the different angles of the thread creates a slightly different color change within the same color of thread.

– – – Try using two different colors of thread in the same needle. Use a larger needle to assure the threads sit comfortably in the groove above the eye. The color variations that result are totally fun! Make sure there is enough difference in value between threads in the same color families or you won't be able to see the difference between the two threads. Using two threads in the same color family gives a "tweedy" look. Stitch a bit slower and a little more carefully with two threads as there is more drag on the eye of the needle.

– – – Try combining a solid color thread with a variegated thread through the needle. The solid color will help to diffuse the variation slightly.

– – – Don't use two threads through one needle when trying to shade and blend. It is impossible to control where the color lands.

SELECTING THE RIGHT THREAD FOR THE JOB

Now armed with a little thread education, let's see how to properly select the right thread for the job at hand. But first, answers to a few questions are in order.

- – – Should 40-weight thread be used for the entire design?
- – – Does the design have intricate or confined areas?
- – – Does the design call for a combination of thread weights?
- – – Do you have the thread colors available to complete the design?
- – – How old are the threads in your stash?

To begin your thread painting adventure, choose simple designs without intricate areas to boost your confidence right away. Although 40-weight thread is the thread of choice for most simple designs, as your thread painting adventure progresses, a combination of weights will result in a more professional design.

Next, inventory your thread stash and determine if you possess the appropriate thread colors needed for the job. Also, evaluate the thread stash and mentally decide if any thread is outdated.

Most of us who have quilted, sewed, or embroidered for a while have a relatively large stash of thread; we assume that it will last forever. Thread manufactured years ago did have a relatively short shelf life but threads manufactured today have an extended shelf life. Longevity in thread not only varies from manufacturer to manufacturer, but also is determined on how the thread is stored.

There is a simple test to determine if thread is still usable. Unwind about 12" and holding the thread firmly in each hand, give it a firm tug. Outdated thread snaps right away. Good quality thread will break too, but it takes a bit more effort. Outdated thread can be a bear to work with because it constantly breaks and frays and will drive you nuts. Should the thread life of a spool be suspect, test the thread in a sample hoop. If it breaks and frays, find another thread.

Start with a simple design such as the fall tree shown in figure 2-3. There are no intricate areas and the thread painting is fairly straightforward. A 40-weight thread would be a good choice for the job. The poppies in figure 2-4, even though small, can be thread painted with a 40-weight thread because there are no detailed areas needing special attention. The pansies in figure 2-5 are the same, again no detail. You get the picture!!

Combining thread weights is the next natural step in thread painting proficiency. Several years ago when I was thread painting the sample for the horse's head in LONGING FOR THE PAST (see page 8-9), I first used a 40-weight choice to thread paint the details around the horse's mouth. The weight of the thread was too heavy for these delicate areas and no space was left to define the lips and nostrils. Plus, two more colors were needed and there was no space left for any more thread. I experimented with a 100-weight thread in the crucial small areas and a 60-weight thread to fill in around them. These thinner threads allowed me the time and space I needed to define the tiny areas in order to give the design realism (see figure 2-6).

Another area where a thinner weight thread works better is the hand on the lady in figure 2-7. The hand is small (1¼") and detailed. To achieve the realism I wanted, three shades of pink, one of yellow, and one of gray were chosen in 100-weight thread. Five shades of thread in such a confining area is a lot, but the thinness of the thread allowed me the space between threads I needed. Had I used a 40-weight thread, two thread colors would have filled up the area and the final design would not have looked

realistic at all. The lesson: Use 60- or 100-weight polyester in small detailed areas with little surface area or for intricate designs. The realism of the design is in the attention to its detail.

Figure 2-6
Horse's head from LONGING FOR THE PAST, *pages 8-9*

SELECTING THREAD BRANDS

Convenience is a great motivating factor when determining the thread brands we select, so we tend to purchase threads available at our local sewing machine, quilt, or fabric shop. However, if you live in a small town and thread variety is not great, a wealth of thread can be found on the Internet. Buy from reputable sites or dealers and avoid the "too good to be true" scenario. In thread you get what you pay for, so avoid bargain brands. Find brands you like that are reliable and stick with them. At the same time, always be on the lookout for what is new and might just add that spark to your project. Regional or national quilt shows are great sources to check out what might be new on the market.

Figure 2-7
Lady's hand detail from LIFE IN HOLLY RIDGE, *pages 6-7*

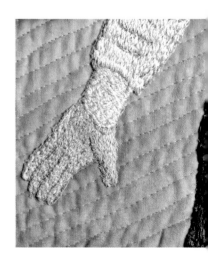

*Figure 2-8
Dots on
thread racks*

DISPLAYING AND ORGANIZING THREADS

The majority of my thread is organized on thread racks by weight and color family. Keeping thread by weights and types minimizes pulling the wrong thread. Thinner 60- and 100-weight threads are kept together by color; variegated threads are stored by color, then weight. At a glance, over 500 spools are available for immediate selection. The ArtBin® Super Satchel™ Series is a great way to store threads, too, because it takes up a minimum amount of space, and, with wheels attached, it can be moved about as needed.

In order to assure each spool is returned to the proper rack spindle, I write the color number of the thread on a colored dot and stick it on the end of the spindle when the thread is removed (see figure 2-8). Once I am through with that color, I remove the dot from the spindle and then stick the dot back on top of the thread which goes back on the spindle. I have a companion thread chart that corresponds to each thread on the rack.

I know you are thinking, "This lady has thread on the brain," but trust me: In the long run, you will know where each thread is when you need it. To help maintain the life of the thread, keep thread racks out of sunny areas. To prolong the life of the thread, cover racks with dark fabric to keep the sun and dust off.

STACKED OR CROSSWOUND THREAD

Most thread is wound on spools in one of two ways—either stacked or crosswound. Crosswound thread is spun so that the thread crosses diagonally over itself and feeds best coming off the top of the spool; use the vertical spindle on your sewing machine. The thread on a stacked spool is wound so the threads are stacked on top of each other. These threads feed best if they come off the side of the spool; use the horizontal spindle.

ORGANIZING THREAD SELECTIONS

For convenience and ease of use, organize the selected thread for a particular design right beside your machine. Thread can be organized in a small container or you can purchase a thread caddy that either attaches to the back of your machine or is freestanding. If the thread is lined up in stitching order, when you repeat the same stitching order again, you don't have to figure out the lineup. Having the threads organized makes changing thread colors a breeze and is a huge time saver when the design has a number of thread colors.

Being an educated thread consumer saves time, money, and a ton of frustration. Plus, the completed thread-painted design will look like it could just walk right off the quilt. There are no shortcuts in thread painting and the bottom line is that it can be time consuming. So make your thread selections wisely, pay attention to the details, avoid the temptation to hurry the process, and you will have a completed design so worth the effort.

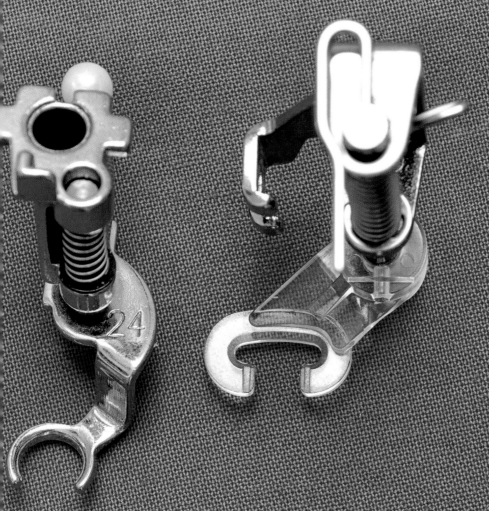

Thread Painting

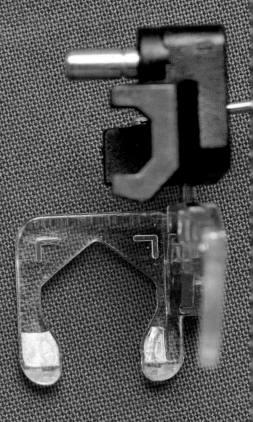

Figure 3-1 Examples of free-motion feet

Supplies

Remember that only straight and zigzag stitches are required in thread painting. I must admit that the newer machines are easier to manipulate, but that older machine can still stitch a mean thread-painted design. In the free-motion stitching used in thread painting the feed dogs are dropped, but if you cannot drop the feed dogs, not to worry; there is a solution for that.

THE SEWING MACHINE

Feed Dogs

With the feed dogs dropped, the hoop can freely move underneath the needle. For machines that do not have the ability to drop the feed dogs, turn the stitch length to 0; the feed dogs will barely move. Another suggestion is to cut a piece of plastic the size of the throat plate, cut a hole for the needle, tape the plastic down, and you are ready to stitch (I have used the thin plastic file folders are made of). A special plate can be purchased to cover the feed dogs, but these tend to inhibit the hoop from moving freely.

Machine Feet

In thread painting it is necessary to see where you have been, where you are, and where you are getting ready to go. An open-toe free-motion foot is a must for stress-free thread painting. An open-toe free-motion foot is just that—an open visible area. A clear oval foot is available for some machines, but visibility with this type of foot is practically zero. Many of my students confuse an open-toe free-motion foot with an open-toe appliqué foot. A free-motion foot will hover above the throat plate when the presser foot is down; a standard presser foot such as the open-toe appliqué foot will sit flat on the throat plate. Check with your machine dealer if you are not familiar with free-motion feet. See figure 3-1.

Upper Tension

The proper tension on the thread coming through the upper thread guide and from the bobbin case is paramount for a realistic design. The most common problem is that the bobbin thread pokes its pesky head to the surface of the design. The first way to eliminate this problem if you have a machine equipped with a finger or hook on the bobbin case is to thread the hole on the end of the finger. Threading the finger creates drag on the thread coming out of the bobbin case, preventing or eliminating the thread from coming to the surface. Many times this is not enough adjustment, so the upper tension will have to be adjusted as well.

With all the specialty threads available today it is imperative that you know how to adjust the upper and lower (bobbin) tensions. Most new machine tensions are calibrated with a tighter tension for general sewing (not thread painting, quilting, or embroidery) that has been preset for a 50- or 60-weight thread. See your service manual to learn how to override the automatic tension to loosen the top tension until you get the stitch quality you desire.

A control dial, wheel, button, or touch screen command on today's machines regulates the upper tension. Most control dials are numbered from 0–10. Rotating the dial towards 0 loosens the tension; rotating the dial towards 10 increases the tension. Computerized on-screen commands vary from 0 to 10 or a plus or minus sign, with a plus sign increasing the tension and a minus sign loosening the tension. If neither threading the finger nor adjusting the top tension corrects the problem, then the bobbin case will have to be adjusted.

Bobbin Tension

Sewing machines come equipped with either a plastic top-loading or metal front-loading bobbin case. For free-motion stitching, more tension needs to be placed on the thread winding out of the bobbin case to create more drag on the thread.

Front-loading Bobbin Cases

On the side of some front-loading bobbin cases is a tension band with two screws. The screw at the end of the band holds the case together while the larger screw regulates the flow of thread. To increase the tension on the thread, turn the larger screw clockwise; to decrease the tension, turn the larger screw counterclockwise (remember—righty tighty, lefty loosey). Be extremely careful when loosening this screw as it is only $1/8$" (3mm) long. Tighten the tension in small increments until the stitch balances out.

The bobbin case that came with your machine was calibrated for your machine and you might want to purchase an extra bobbin case if you are not confident adjusting the tension. Mark the adjusted bobbin case with a dot of fingernail polish so you will know which bobbin case has been adjusted. But if you are confident adjusting your bobbin case, mark the location of the original setting with a thin line of polish on either side of the screw indention. This way the screw can be adjusted back to its original setting.

Top-loading Bobbin

The tension screw for top-loading bobbin cases in most machines is located on the top or side of the housing. Remove the housing and mark the location of the original setting with fingernail polish. Turn the screw to the right in small increments to tighten the tension. An extra housing can be purchased for many top-loading machines. Mark the housing with polish so you know it is the adjusted bobbin case.

Some embroidery machines, whether front- or top-loading, come with a special bobbin case calibrated for embroidery. Drag has been placed on the thread winding out of the bobbin, which helps

A few tips to remember when working with your machine

— — — The presser foot should always be up when threading the machine to allow the thread to fall between the tension disks. Once the foot is lowered, the disks close, exerting tension on the thread to assure the proper stitch. Should the thread bypass the tension disks (which could happen when threading with the foot down), there is no tension on the needle thread, resulting in loops forming underneath the design or fabric.

— — — Should bobbin thread suddenly appear on the surface of the design when everything was humming along nicely, check to see if the thread has become tangled around the spindle. If caught there, the thread cannot flow through the needle, resulting in the bobbin thread being pulled to the surface of the design.

— — — Should a blob of thread form underneath the hoop, check to see if the presser foot is down. Since the open-toe free-motion presser foot hovers, it is easy to neglect lowering it.

— — — Incorrect threading can cause a rat's nest underneath either the design or the throat plate. Rethreading may solve the problem.

— — — The bobbin tension is too tight if the top thread shows on the back and too loose if the bobbin thread is looped on the back.

— — — And finally, keep your machine clean and serviced for maximum performance. Make it a routine to clean and oil your machine after every 3-4 bobbins or every 6-8 hours of use. Check your owner's manual for maintenance procedures.

keep the thread from showing on the surface. This bobbin case can be adjusted as well.

Recently serviced machines may need no adjusting to regulate the top and bobbin tension, so before adjusting either the top or bottom tension, do some practice stitching to check the stitch quality. You may not need to make any adjustments at all.

The bottom line is to read your manual to make sure you are adjusting the upper and lower tensions correctly. Thread painting does take a bit of time, and thread isn't cheap, so you want to make sure your machine is performing to its utmost capacity to assure you of perfect stitches.

Needles

Needles are one of the single most important yet least expensive items needed for successful thread painting. I had a misguided workshop student tell me with pride that she only changed her needle when it broke. Needles take a lot of abuse during thread painting due to the high stitch density of some designs. The constant penetration of the needle into the design can dull or burr the needle, causing missed stitches and poor stitch quality. Thread shredding and consistent thread breakage can both be needle related, so to keep frustration to a minimum, change the needle often. Even a new needle straight out of the package can have a small deformity, so discard it right away should it not stitch correctly.

The type and brand of needle you prefer is a personal choice, but for thread painting, give Schmetz Microtex sharp or topstitch needles a try. Both are dependable and come in an assortment of sizes.

– – – Use a 60/8 or 70/10 for creating fine, detailed lines in confined spaces and for delicate facial features. This needle is very fragile, so use it with a higher weight thread (thinner) and be aware that most of the machines equipped with a needle threader will not thread a 60/8 needle.

– – – Use a 80/12 for light- to medium-density stitch designs, the category into which most thread-painted deigns fall. Use a 90/14 needle to penetrate high-density stitch designs needing some "punching" power.

– – – Be sure to use a metallic needle when using metallic thread. As metallic thread passes through the eye of the needle, it creates friction, which creates heat at the eye. Metallic needles have been Teflon®-coated to help reduce this heat buildup, which can cause the thread to break.

– – – Another needle to consider is a titanium needle. This needle is a little more expensive but it lasts 5 to 8 times longer than a standard needle. It comes in an assortment of sizes.

– – – On the back side of the needle above the eye there is a groove the thread needs to fit into. If the thread is too small or too thick for this grove, skipped stitches can occur. Also, the thread can fray if the eye of the needle is too small for the thread.

SETTING UP THE STUDIO

A few of the supplies necessary for thread painting may be unfamiliar to you or, in some cases, might not be readily available. Supplies necessary for thread painting or sketching are fairly simple—some stabilizer, a little tulle, a hoop, and you're ready to thread paint. Add batting, art supplies, and a few notions, and you can rock and roll.

Stabilizer

Stabilizer acts as the foundation for a thread-painted design much like the foundation does for a house; if properly selected, it helps to maintain the integrity of the finished product. The stabilizer along with the correct hoop and underlay stitch supports the fabric to minimize movement and ensures that the design stitches properly. Stabilizer effectively minimizes shrinkage and distortion. The stabilizer of choice for the majority of my thread designs is a water-soluble stabilizer (clear) film or water-soluble stabilizer (white) backing (see figure 3-2).

Water-Soluble Stabilizer Film

Water-soluble stabilizer film is clear and comes in an assortment of different weights. While any of the different weights can be used, for maximum results use a heavier type. I prefer Dissolve-4X™ stabilizer made by Superior Threads; it is heavy but pliable, can withstand numerous needle penetrations, and washes away easily. The design is drawn onto the film which acts as a stitching guide for either the Tulle Sandwich or Direct method (see pages 37 and 41, respectively).

The stabilizer should be cut at least 2" larger on all 4 sides of the drawn design to assure ease in reaching the outer edges of the design, i.e., cut the stabilizer 14" for a 10" square design.

Water-soluble stabilizer film comes in a plastic covering or bag. Once removed, the film is affected by conditions in the air. In moist, humid climates, it will absorb moisture, making the stabilizer soft and flimsy. At dry high altitudes or in heated areas, the moisture in the stabilizer is removed, making it brittle. Both conditions are difficult to work with. To prevent either scenario, place the unused portion of the stabilizer film back in its original packaging or in an airtight plastic bag. Should the stabilizer dry out, place it in a dry area away from any direct moisture in the shower area, turn on the hot water, close the door for a bit, and the moisture will be absorbed back into the stabilizer.

Water-Soluble Stabilizer Backing

White water-soluble stabilizer backing is used in both the Tulle Sandwich and Direct methods. In the Tulle Sandwich it is used as the bottom layer. Because the stabilizer is semi-opaque, it creates a visual barrier between the design and the throat plate, making it much easier to see the design lines. Clear water-soluble stabilizer film can be used as the bottom layer, but because it is clear, seeing the design lines is a little more difficult.

Water-soluble stabilizer backing is also used in the Direct method. Two layers are positioned underneath the fabric to support it while thread painting, but once the design is completed, the stabilizer is easily washed away. I prefer Aqua Mesh manufactured by OESD, which can be found at any BERNINA store. This temporary stabilizer looks and feels like fabric and is lightweight but stable enough to handle high-density designs. Two layers normally do the trick, but more can be used if necessary. Aqua Magic by Pfaff and Wet N Gone by Floriani are two other suitable stabilizer backings. Water-soluble stabilizer film and backing can be found at most sewing machine stores or on the Internet.

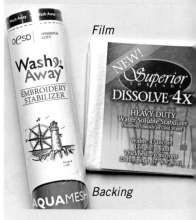

Figure 3-2
Photo of stabilizers

Figure 3-3
Large canopy
detail from
LIFE IN HOLLY
RIDGE, *pages 6-7*

Tear-away Stabilizer

Tear-away stabilizer has its limitations in thread painting, but is used in the Direct method in larger designs. Tear-away is a little more difficult to position in the hoop because it is stiffer and less pliable than water-soluble. The number of layers of tear-away depends on the density of the design; a single layer of medium-weight tear-away should be adequate for most medium-density designs.

The canopy in LIFE IN HOLLY RIDGE, pages 6-7 and figure 3-3, was approximately 12" x 12", which by thread painting standards is a very large canopy, especially when thread painting directly onto fabric. I used 3 layers of water-soluble stabilizer backing, which seemed to do an adequate job until I washed the stabilizer away. Once washed, there was nothing permanent to hold the hundreds of thousands of stitches together and the canopy collapsed. A stabilizer that remained with the completed canopy would have eliminated the problem.

To remove the stabilizer, cut away the excess to within 2" of the design. Then cut or tear away the remaining stabilizer to the edge of the stitching. Along unstable edges, put pressure on the outside edge of the stitching with your finger or small ruler to minimize damage to the fragile stitches as you tear.

Tulle

Tulle (bridal veil) is a very fine polyester or nylon net with tiny holes. Tulle is used between the layers of stabilizer in the Tulle Sandwich method and is the backbone that assures the completed thread appliqué is solid and stable. Tulle can be found at most fabric stores. Select gray or silver; these colors work well with any thread colors.

Hoops

Many different sizes and types of machine embroidery hoops are available ranging from 6" to 10". It would seem that the larger the hoop, the better. The problem is that the larger the hoop, the greater the distortion. Plus, larger hoops constantly hit the head of the machine, which will drive you nuts. Choose a 6" machine embroidery hoop to keep the area to be thread painted under constant tension. The hoop helps keep distortion under control, resulting in a more professional product.

My hoop of choice is a 6" wooden machine embroidery hoop (see figure 3-4). Benefits from using this little workhorse include:

- − − $^1/_4$" sides—this assures the hoop will fit under most presser feet
- − − − a solid inner ring
- − − − a strong outer ring with a heavy-duty screw assembly equipped with an indentation for a screw driver so you can add extra torque to secure high-density designs
- − − − surface tension can be increased

Plastic and spring hoops are also available. In neither of these hoops can the tension be adjusted inside the hoop, which results in less stabilization. The benefit to the plastic hoop is that it has a strong screw assembly; the disadvantage is that the sides are higher, making it difficult to slide under some presser feet. The spring hoop has a plastic outer ring and a metal inner ring with handles at each end. The disadvantage to this hoop is that it is not strong enough to use with denser designs and does not keep the stabilizer under constant tension.

When thread painting, two hoops are needed—one for the thread painting design and one to use to test thread colors or make samples. It is just too much trouble to remove the working design from the hoop each time practice stitches are needed or to audition new thread colors.

The bottom line is that the 6" wooden hoop is strong, stable, lasts forever, and offers the proper stabilization to help assure a distortion-free design. Thread painting, while easy, is time–consuming, so don't shortcut the final results by using an inferior hoop.

Batting

Batting seems to be a personal decision and we all have that perfect batting we prefer. Thread-painted quilts are not among the "snuggle" variety and due to their stiff nature, they are normally used for wallhangings.

My preference is a batting with no stretch on the crosswise or lengthwise grains. A medium fleece, fusible or non-fusible, stays pliable but is still firm enough to accommodate heavy or light quilting, plus, once quilted, is stable enough to offer a sturdy backing for the thread appliqués. Fusible fleece works well if there is any distortion on the quilt top; the excess fabric created by distortion can be eased in during fusing.

Art Supplies

A few art supplies are recommended for thread painting (see figure 3-5). To trace the design onto a piece of water-soluble stabilizer film, purchase an ultra-fine point Sharpie® marker or a Micron® Pigma® pen. The plus to Micron Pigma pens is they come in an assortment of point sizes from .005 to 8.0mm and they come in a variety of colors. To trace the design, select a 1.0-2.0 size. Using different color pens, designs can be color-coded to alert you to a thread-color change.

Should you want to augment your quilts with colored ink, try Tsukineko® inks. They are just way too much fun to play with, and of all the paints and inks I have tried, they are the most user-friendly. The inks come in a 15mm bottle and are applied with either a round or pointed Fantastix™ brush. Simply rub off most of the ink, test on a practice piece, and you are ready to go. A diagonal shader paint brush can also be used to ink the designs, making it easier to get the edge of the brush into small corners and tight spaces. These inks are colorfast and permanent.

Additional Notions

– – – A tilt tray for your machine helps reduce the tension in your back and shoulder area. A good substitute is to place a rubberized drawer liner under the sewing machine and position 2 rubber door stops evenly apart under the back of the machine.

– – – A stencil cutter is a must when thread painting (see figure 3-6). Use it to remove the tulle from finished thread appliqués. The beauty of the stencil cutter is that it literally melts the polyester thread or nylon tulle away, while fusing the edge of the thread to create a strong, solid edge. A stencil cutter can be found online or at craft stores.

– – – Removable tape is used to secure the pattern to the water-soluble stabilizer film. It is one of the few tapes that can be removed successfully without creating a hole in the stabilizer. Removable tape can be found at most office supply and craft stores.

– – – Use a rounded-blade scissors for best results. The rounded blade cuts the thread right down to the surface, eliminating any frayed edges.

Figure 3-4
6" hoops

Figure 3-5
Art supplies

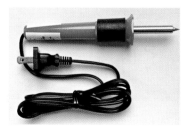

Figure 3-6
Stencil cutter

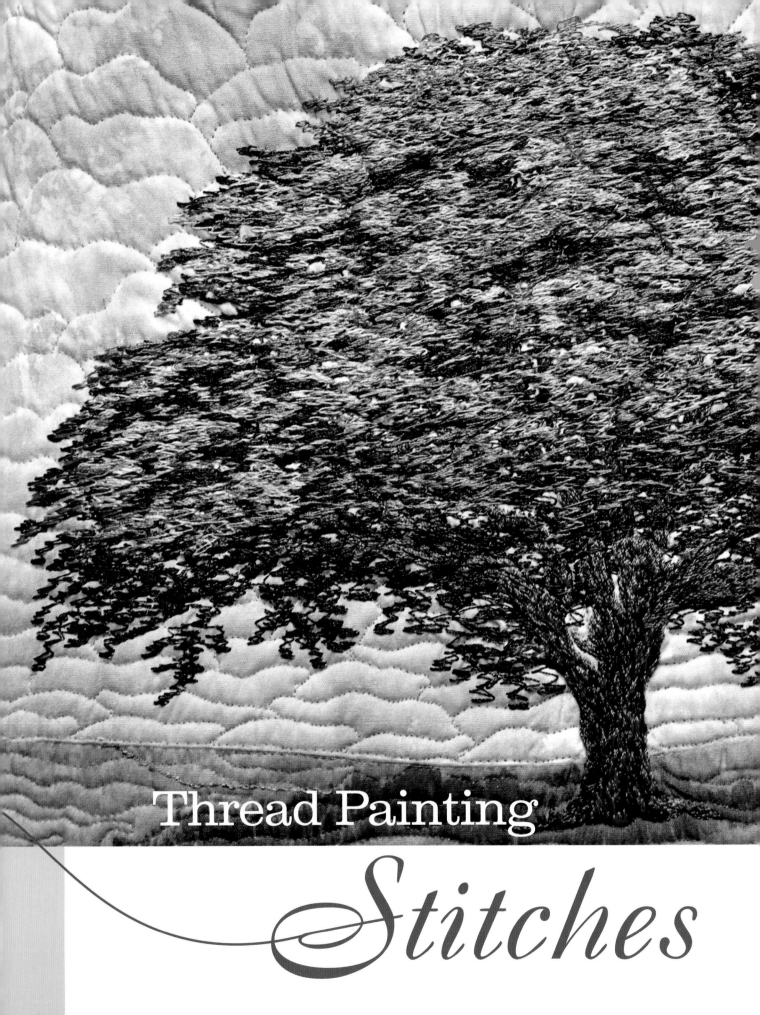

Thread Painting
Stitches

Thread Painting with Style   NANCY PRINCE

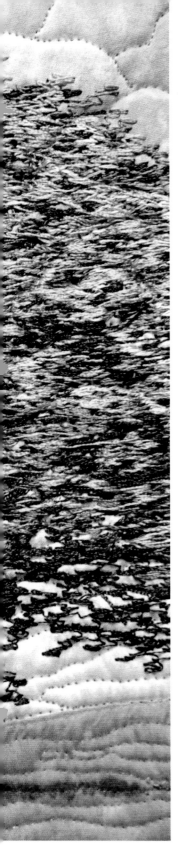

Straight or zigzag stitches are the only stitches I use in thread painting. Use a wider (3.5-4.5mm) zigzag stitch for designs with wide open spaces and a narrower (1.0-2.5mm) width for confined areas. Use a straight stitch for smaller, more confining spaces and for areas that need more control.

Smooth, controlled movements of the hoop and a constant, even machine speed determine the stitch length when free-motion stitching, so the stitch length on your machine doesn't have to be adjusted at all. With the feed dogs dropped, you control the length of the stitch by how fast or slow the hoop is moved or how fast or slow the machine is running. The speed of the hoop or machine is not as important as developing a rhythm that is right for you. What changes the look of the stitch depends on how the hoop is moved and whether a straight or zigzag stitch is used.

Following are descriptions of the thread painting stitches I use. Having a name for a specific stitch simplifies pattern directions later in the book. There are an infinite number of hoop movements; those described are just the ones I use most often.

UNDER THE SPREADING...,
15" x 15", made by the author

UNDERLAY STITCH – THE FOUNDATION

The underlay stitch is used to support and stabilize medium- to high-stitch density designs and is used in designs over $3/8"$ in diameter. Designs less than $3/8"$ wide do not require underlay stitches because there is not enough thread density in such small areas to create distortion.

Always sewn perpendicular to the fill stitches, the underlay stitch helps minimize distortion and shrinkage. It doesn't have to be pretty; it just needs to get the job done. Also, the underlay stitch helps bind the layers together to keep them from moving independently from each other; this results in less distortion and puckering as the thread-painted stitches are applied.

Use the straight stitch for underlay; it works better than the zigzag because the stitches are closer together, resulting in a more stable design.

The underlay stitch is used to stabilize designs in both the Tulle Sandwich and the Direct methods. Distortion outside the design using the Tulle Sandwich method will simply be cut away and no one will be the wiser that it was ever there. However, distortion outside the design stitched directly onto fabric or the quilt

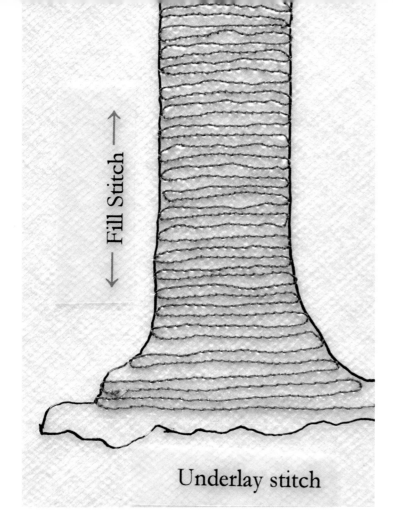

Fill Stitch

Underlay stitch

Figure 4-1
Underlay of trunk showing arrow for fill stitches

Figure 4-2
Note the different directions of the underlay stitch.

top will show. Small amounts of distortion can be quilted out with your fingers and thus eliminated, but larger amounts are there to stay and can be an unsightly mess after quilting. So plan ahead!

Underlay stitches are paramount to a distortion-free design. Having said that, distortion can still occur in high-density stitch designs even if the underlay stitches are properly stitched and the design is hooped and stabilized correctly. Distortion can never be completely eliminated, but by using the proper stabilizing techniques it can be minimized.

Because underlay stitches are stitched in place before thread painting the design, it is imperative to think about the final fill stitch first. In all cases the underlay stitch is perpendicular to the final fill stitch. For example, in figure 4-1 you know that most bark on a tree runs up the trunk (or north), so the underlay stitches need to run east to west across the tree.

Within a design some underlay stitches might be going in one direction and others in a completely opposite direction. Look at the flower petals in figure 4-2. For the underlay stitches to be perpendicular to the final fill stitch, rotate the hoop so each petal faces you to execute the stitch. Insert the needle at the bottom right of the design, then stitch to the left side. With the machine still running, stitch north about $1/8$", then stitch back to the right side of the design. Stitch north and repeat the rows up the trunk (see figures 4-1 and 4-2).

Figure 4-3
Snowmen showing invisible
and solid thread to underlay

To underlay most small designs where there are no design lines inside the design (see figure 4-1), use the first thread painting color. For more intricate designs where it is important to be able to see specific interior design lines, use Superior's MonoPoly invisible thread. In figure 4-3, clear invisible thread was used to underlay the left snowman, making it easy to see the interior design lines. On the right snowman a darker thread was used for the underlay, making it more difficult to see the interior design lines.

Tip: *In larger designs that require two or more hoopings, underlay the entire design before beginning to thread paint. The vertical distance between the underlay lines is only about $1/8$", making it difficult for distortion to occur in such a small space. The large amount of underlay makes it more difficult for distortion to occur inside and outside the perimeter of the design. In designs this large, use an invisible thread to underlay the design to avoid covering up the design lines within the design.*

Figure 4-4
*Execution of
straight stitch*

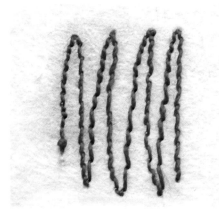 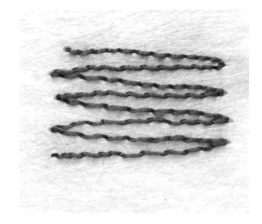

STRAIGHT STITCH – THE DEFINER

In addition to being used as the underlay stitch, the straight stitch is used as a fill stitch. It subtly highlights or shades a design and helps blend one thread into another. It is also used to define a design's shape; when the design calls for a more compact, flat appearance; and when more control is needed. Small confining areas also require a straight stitch.

To execute the straight stitch, maintain an even speed and move the hoop in slow, controlled movements. The straight stitch remains a straight stitch no matter how the hoop is rotated. The needle only moves up and down, so to change the look of the stitch, move the hoop in different directions.

The best way to understand this is to hoop a piece of muslin and stabilizer and practice just moving the hoop around. You will see very quickly that no matter how the hoop is rotated, the stitch look is the same. Notice in figure 4-4 that when the hoop is moved north to south, vertical lines are stitched. Rotate the hoop a quarter of a turn and move the hoop east to west and the look remains the same. The lines, even though they are going in different directions, stitch out the same.

The straight stitch is also used as a reverse eraser. Many times when beginning a thread painting, some stray stitches I call "hiccups" appear on the outside edges of solid designs. It can be too difficult to remove these stragglers, so position the needle at the hiccup and move the hoop in short parallel movements along the edge of the design in the direction of the original stitches. This will blend in the stragglers so they become part of the design.

ZIGZAG STITCH – THE WORKHORSE

The zigzag stitch is used in about 95 percent of all my thread work. It's more versatile than the straight stitch because its width can be changed from 0 to 4.5mm, plus it fills in much faster than the straight stitch. The zigzag stitch creates more dimension than the straight stitch due to the space between the zig and zag.

In normal sewing with the feed dogs up, the zigzag stitch only moves vertically, creating a satin stitch. A different look can be obtained by increasing the length between the stitches, but that is just about all that can be done with the feed dogs up. With the feed dogs dropped to

up   down

Figure 4-5
Zigzag stitching with feed dogs up and down

Tip: Remember this one important rule when using the zigzag as a fill stitch: Keep the line you are thread painting parallel to the table edge and you will always have a straight line of stitches. The easiest way to execute this is to concentrate on the line inside the open-toe presser foot.

Figure 4-6
Stitch with the line parallel to you.

allow free-motion sewing, the same compact satin stitch is obtained by slowly pulling the hoop toward you. To increase the space between the satin stitches, pull the hoop faster towards you (see figure 4-5).

Even though the satin stitch has its place in thread painting, the zigzag stitch is used most often as a fill stitch.

To fill the design with a zigzag stitch, run the machine at a comfortable speed and move the hoop slowly east to west—a straight line of stitching will occur. Continue moving the hoop east to west, laying one line of stitches next to another; this fills in the design. As the design arcs to the right or left, rotate the hoop so the line you are thread painting stays parallel to the table edge (see figure 4-6).

To maintain control of the stitch when traveling from a large surface area to a small one, such as from a tree trunk to a smaller branch, reduce the width of the stitch to maintain control. Use short, controlled, right-to-left movements with the hoop to fill in the design. It doesn't matter where you start thread painting within the design, but starting in a wide open area is easier.

Zigzag stitches fill in faster than straight stitches. However, a zigzag stitch can be used in compact areas of a design just by decreasing the stitch width. So, as with the straight stitch, before you begin thread painting, practice first on a sample piece to get comfortable with moving the hoop for the result you want.

Tip: The larger the surface area to thread paint, the wider the zigzag stitch width; the smaller the area, the narrower the width.

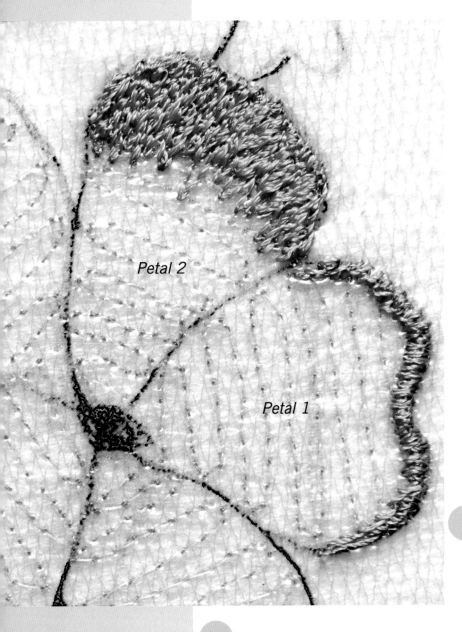

Figure 4-7
Meandering satin
stitches assure
a solid outside
edge in petal 1.
In petal 2,
a zigzag stitch
fills in the re-
maining area of
the design.

For example, notice petal 1 in figure 4-7. A small 2.0mm satin stitch created the meandering column of stitches on the outside edge of the flower petal. On designs such as this it is very difficult to thread paint to the outside edge of the petal and assure a solid edge each time the hoop is moved east to west. To simplify this process, thread paint a line of meandering satin stitches to assure a solid outside edge.

The execution of the satin stitch creates a slightly rounded column of stitches. For some designs this roundness might be just what you want visually, but on the outside edge of other designs, including the flower petal mentioned to the left, this roundness needs to be flattened out so all the stitches are on the same plane. In figure 4-7, petal 2, the hoop was moved east to west using a zigzag stitch not only to flatten the column of stitches so they were not noticeable, but also to fill in the remaining area of the design.

SCRIBBLE STITCH – FREEDOM AND FLEXIBILITY

The scribble stitch is just what we all did as a kid—scribble. This is a free stitch with no bounds, so just have fun with it!

To develop a rhythm for this stitch, try scribbling on paper and then transfer that movement to the hoop. To execute the stitch, set the machine to a straight or zigzag stitch and move the hoop right to left and up and down at the same time. The relationship between the foot speed and the hoop movement determines the length of the stitch.

SATIN STITCH – THE SIMPLIFIER

The satin stitch is always a zigzag stitch and is used when a solid column of stitches is required. I take a bit of creative license when using the word "column" in reference to a satin stitch. Vertical columns of tapering satin stitches are used on evergreen trunks, but mostly the satin stitch in thread painting is used to define the outside edges of some designs to assure they are solid.

It is not necessary to draw the design first for small scribble areas. The tendency is to move the hoop too fast, resulting in broken needles and long loopy stitches, so keep the hoop speed slow even though the pedal speed is fast.

BLENDING STITCH – THE UNIFIER

Thread cannot be mixed or blended together like paint, so it needs to be stitched in place in such a way that the eye does the blending. The blending stitch can be a straight or zigzag stitch and is used anytime it is necessary to combine two or more colors together for a gradual change from one color to another. It is primarily used when the design calls for complete realism such as for clothing, animals, inanimate objects, hair, flowers— the examples are endless. It is a simple, fun stitch and easy to master.

For example, in figure 4-8 the four thread colors were butted against each other so there was no intertwining of threads. The colors are just colors, and while they are harmonious together, visually they offer no excitement and in particular, no realism. It is obvious where one color stops and the next one starts. Now look at figure 4-9; notice that it is difficult to tell where one color stops and the next one starts. This was achieved by carefully blending one color into another using both the zigzag and the sketch stitch.

Execution of the blending stitch is quite easy. Notice in figure 4-10 how the outside edges of the first thread, a pale yellow, were thread painted in a jagged fashion using a zigzag stitch. The uneven jagged edges of the outside edge allows

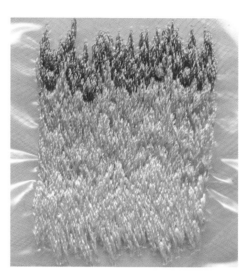

Figure 4-8
Orange poppy colors bumped together

Figure 4-9
Orange poppies blended

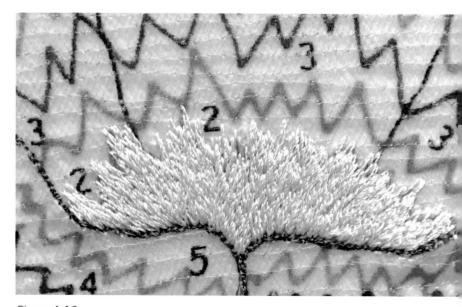

Figure 4-10
Orange poppies color 1

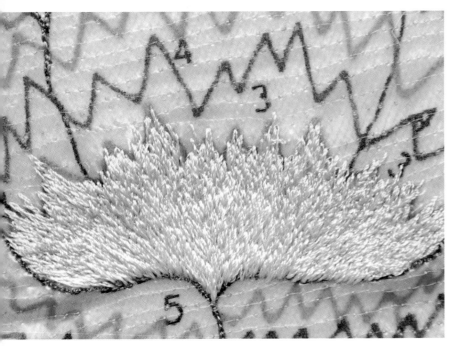

Figure 4-11
Orange poppies color 2

the second thread, a brighter yellow, to blend between the pale yellow stitches already in place (see figure 4-11). As the brighter yellow is thread painted into the pale yellow, notice how the outside edges are very jagged to allow the third yellow to blend in. The remaining colors were thread painted in the same fashion except for the final rust, which bumped to the outside edge, as shown in figure 4-12.

In the example, the zigzag stitches did a great job thread painting the stitches necessary to cover the surface of the drawn design, but they were too heavy to create the final shading and blending required for most designs. The zigzag stitch does all the work but the following sketch stitch gets all the credit for a realistic design.

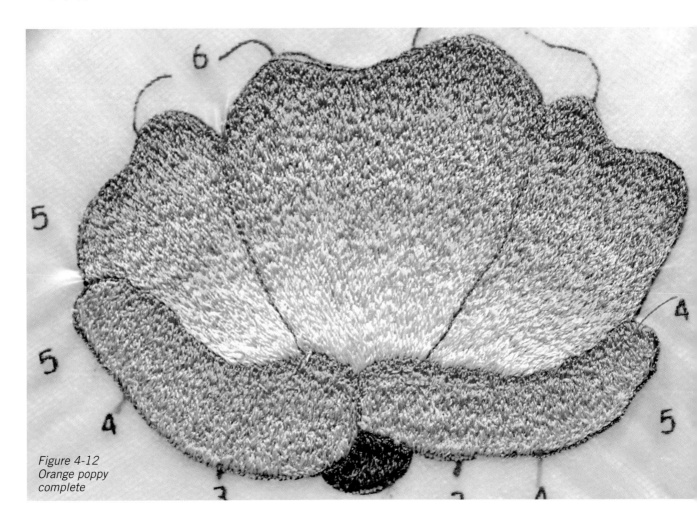

Figure 4-12
Orange poppy complete

SKETCH STITCH – THE FILLER AND BLENDER

Most of the designs to thread paint are stitched using a zigzag stitch, and in the majority of instances, the design will be lying on its side to thread paint the design. The zigzag stitches closest to you are hiding small holes behind them and it is virtually impossible to find and fill in the holes with the design on its side. To visually locate the holes, rotate the design so it is facing you. It is now easy to see any holes that need filling. The easiest way to fill the holes is to make your own sketch stitch using the straight stitch.

To execute the sketch stitch to fill holes, rotate the hoop so the design is facing you. Move the hoop slowly north to south in very short movements to form a stitch that looks something like the left example in figure 4-13. The stitch becomes a type of sketch as you hunt out the holes. This erratic movement fills the holes without changing the look of the design.

In figure 4-14 the red dots indicate the holes in the trunk. The green line shows the sketch made by the thread as it moves from hole to hole to fill. Should the holes happen to be in a row, don't make a straight line of stitches down the design—the stitches will show. However, moving the hoop in a short north-to-south motion fills in the holes nicely and leaves no tell-tale line. Hold the design up to a light before removing it from the hoop to make sure all the holes are filled. Pin-prick holes are okay, but holes you can see with the naked eye should be filled.

The sketch stitch changes into a blending stitch quite easily. As shown in figure 4-11 on page 32, rotate the hoop so the

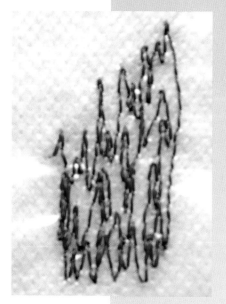

petal is facing you. Move the hoop slowly north to south to allow the thread to fall between the zigzag stitches already in place. This repetitive stitch softens and blends the irregular edges between the two thread colors. This works for any design where blending is required and will be the final stitch before rinsing away the stabilizers.

The sketch stitch is also used as the final stitch when shading is required. Shading gives form to a design and requires a good deal of finesse to create a realistic illusion of depth and shadow. To execute the stitch, rotate the design so it is facing you and literally "sketch" the shading threads into the design by moving the hoop slowly north to south until the shading is dark enough. The fineness of the stitch allows the thread the time necessary to shade the design so it looks real.

Figure 4-13
Sketch stitch filling and shading

Figure 4-14
Trunk with dots showing how to fill holes

Figure 4-15
Shading
on lady's
red coat

The final shading on the lady's coat in figure 4-15 was completed using the sketch stitch. The example on the right in in figure 4-13 on page 33 shows a good rendition of the execution of the stitch at the bottom of the coat. More stitches were required to get the shading dark enough, but the example gives you an idea of what the sketch stitch should look like to complete the final shading on a design.

HOPSCOTCH STITCH – THE DEPTH CREATOR

The hopscotch stitch is used when the design calls for a small concentrated area of color in specific areas—not color throughout a design. On the canopy in UNDER THE SPREADING..., I wanted to give the illusion that the viewer could "see" into the canopy. To achieve this, a zigzag stitch and a dark green thread were required. Remember, a dark color recedes to draw the eye into the canopy (see figure 4-16).

To execute the stitch, rotate the hoop so the design is facing you and move the hoop, right to left, slowly, sewing small, concentrated, irregular areas of thread. Raise the needle and move to another area. Repeat. Continue hopscotching around the design until the specific thread gives you the result you want. Cut the connecting threads when the design is complete or when they get in the way.

Figure 4-16
Hopscotch
stitch in UNDER
THE SPREADING...

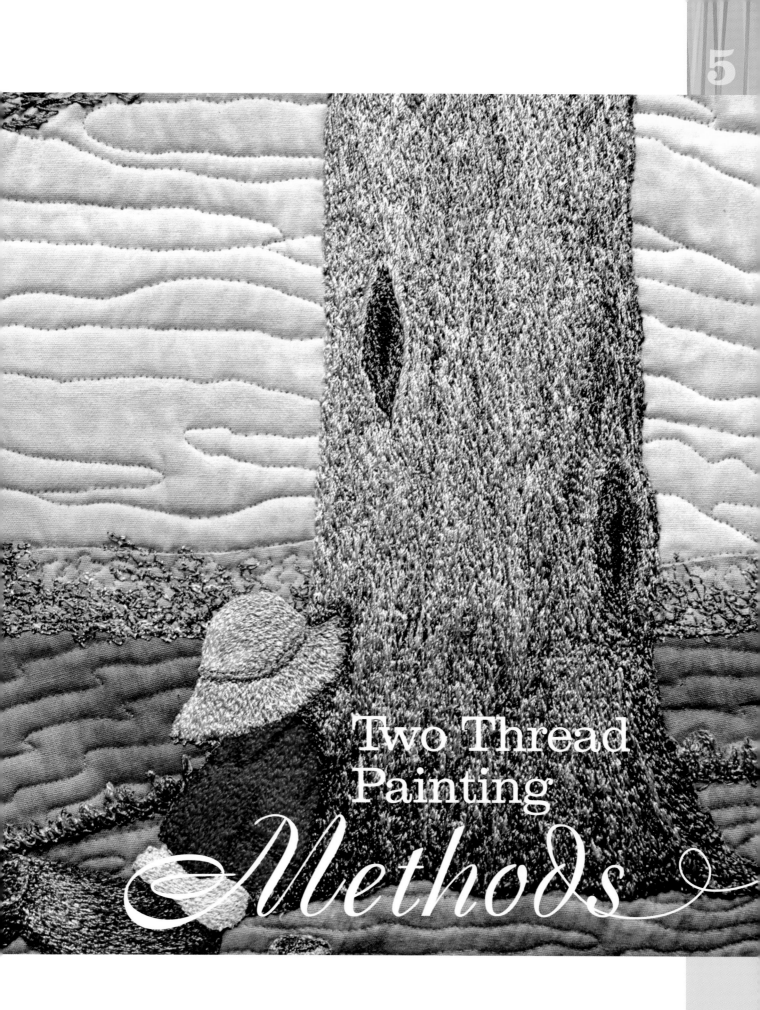

Two Thread Painting *Methods*

Figure 5-1
Large tree trunk
with distortion

There are two thread painting methods I use. The first method, and the one I use most often, is thread painting on the Tulle Sandwich. Once the design is complete on the Tulle Sandwich, the resulting thread-painted appliqué is attached to the quilt. The second method is thread painting directly onto the fabric to be used in the quilt.

Before the two methods can be discussed in detail, you need to be fortified with a little knowledge on how distortion affects a design. Distortion is the altering, changing, or twisting out of shape of the thread-painted design or the surrounding fabric or stabilizer. Distortion appears as ripples in the design or puckers along the edges. It is caused by the force exerted on the surrounding fibers as thread enters the fabric or stabilizer. The more stitches introduced into a confined area, the less room available and the more force created. This force causes the fabric or stabilizer to shrink in the direction of the stitching and stretch in the opposite direction.

In figure 5-1, distortion created by using the Tulle Sandwich method is apparent around the outside edges of the tree trunk. However, once the stabilizer is trimmed and washed away as shown in figure 5-2, the distortion disappears; the end result is a solid flat edge. In contrast, if the same trunk were to be thread painted directly onto fabric, the distortion created around the outside edge of the design would be permanent; no amount of quilting would ever eliminate the ripples in the fabric. For more on distortion, see chapter 8 on page 55.

Figure 5-2
Large tree trunk cleaned up

TULLE SANDWICH METHOD

The Tulle Sandwich method consists of sandwiching two pieces of tulle or bridal veil between two pieces of water-soluble stabilizer. A permanent marker is used to trace the design onto a clear stabilizer used as the top layer. The resulting drawing is an easy reference and becomes the guide to thread paint the design. Without this drawing, it would just be a visual guess as to where the stitches should be thread painted. The tulle acts as an insurance policy to assure the design remains stable once the stabilizers are washed away.

To use the Tulle Sandwich method, the outside edges of the design must be stable enough so they can be cut out. Generally, that means a high-stitch density design, i.e., the design contains a large number of stitches in a small area. Examples include tree trunks, large flowers, animals, inanimate objects, and people. The design itself does not have to be large—just a lot of stitches in a confined space.

I use the Tulle Sandwich method in about 95 percent of my designs because it allows me a sense of freedom; if a mistake is made, it won't be costly. Plus, since they are freestanding units, I have the flexibility to move the completed thread appliqués around on the quilt top until I am satisfied with their location.

Tracing and Hooping the Design

1 Select the design to thread paint. Tape the pattern to a flat surface.

2 Cut out 1 piece of clear water-soluble stabilizer film and 1 (2 for Direct method) piece of water-soluble stabilizer backing (the white stabilizer) the size of the design plus 2" extra on all 4 sides.

3 Line up the center of the clear stabilizer film with the center of the design and secure in place with a piece of removable tape. Use a fine tip permanent black marker to trace the design. This drawing becomes the guide to thread paint the design, so be accurate!

4 Write your name on the stabilizer near where the thread painting will begin to indicate the right side. The drawing looks the same from both sides, so without some indication of which side is which, it is easy to thread paint a mirror image of the design.

5 Cut 2 pieces of gray or silver tulle the size of the stabilizer (Omit this step for Direct method.)

6 On a flat surface, layer the white stabilizer backing, then the tulle, and finally the drawn stabilizer on top. (For the Direct method, use 2 pieces of white stabilizer backing, add the fabric or quilt top without any tulle, and place the clear stabilizer on top.)

7 While standing, unscrew the hoop screw and slide the outer ring underneath all layers with the screw assembly at 6 o'clock. This will assist you in locating the screw in step 9.

8 Following figure 5-3, push the inner ring inside the outer ring on top of all

Figure 5-3 Straightening the top stabilizer

layers, keeping your fingertips on the inner ring. Gently pull the top stabilizer to remove any ripples inside the hoop. Grip the stabilizer close to the edge of the hoop. Work your way around the hoop pulling on the stabilizer until most of the ripples are gone, keeping pressure with your fingertips on the inside ring. Normally ripples appear only on the top stabilizer, but if necessary, while still holding down the inner ring, repeat the process on the bottom stabilizer to remove any ripples.

9 Keeping your fingers on the inner ring, slide the hoop to the edge of the table and tighten the screw about 90 percent.

10 Evaluate the stabilizer and adjust it if necessary until no more ripples are apparent.

11 Tighten the screw all the way down. If ripples remain, back off the screw, readjust the stabilizer and tighten the screw again.

12 Pick up the hoop, and with your thumbs, press down on the inner ring until about 1/8" of the inner ring shows on the back side (see figure 5-4). This adds extra tension on the stabilizer. The bottom of the stabilizer should sit slightly below the outer ring.

*Figure 5-4
Back side of hoop showing 1/8" of stabilizer extending*

13 Pin any excess tulle (or fabric for Direct method) and stabilizer toward the hoop to prevent it from getting caught underneath.

14 To begin thread painting, pull the bobbin thread to the surface, secure a few stitches, and cut the thread tails.

Removing the Stabilizer

1 Cut the excess tulle and stabilizer away to within 1/2" of the design's outer edges.

2 Run warm or cold water over the design to wash the "goo" away as the stabilizer breaks down (check manufacturer's recommendations for water temperature). Use your fingers to work out the residue until it is gone.

3 Rub bar or liquid soap into both sides of the thread appliqué with your fingers. The soap helps break down the stabilizer trapped inside the design.

4 Fill a bowl or sink with cold or warm water to which you have added some fabric softener (about 1 part fabric softener to 4 parts water) and let the thread appliqué soak. The fabric softener helps to soften the thread appliqué.

5 From time to time rub the thread appliqué between your thumb and forefinger; if it is tacky, change the water/ fabric softener and let it soak longer. It is difficult to calculate the exact time necessary to soak out the stabilizer, as that is determined by the stitch density; the higher the density, the longer it will take.

6 Blot and allow to air dry.

7 Block the thread appliqué: 1) place a pressing cloth down; 2) turn the thread

Figure 5-5
Removing the
tulle with a
stencil cutter

appliqué face-side down; 3) place another pressing cloth on top; 4) spritz with water and steam to set the thread appliqué.

Removing the Tulle

There are two ways to remove the tulle. One is by cutting away the tulle with a sharp pair of scissors. My preferred way is to use a stencil cutter (see figure 5-5). To do this:

1 Attach the sharp tip to the stencil cutter and plug it in.

2 Lay the thread appliqué right-side up on a piece of glass, an old tile, or a plate. Run the hot tip of the stencil cutter around the outside edge of the appliqué. Like magic, the tulle will disappear.

3 The residue from the tulle can collect on the tip of the stencil cutter, so use an old cloth to wipe it away every minute or so.

4 Keep the tip moving. Resting in one place can make a hole along the edge.

As the heat from the tip of the stencil cutter runs around the edge of the polyester or rayon thread, it slightly fuses the edge of the thread appliqué creating a very strong, solid edge. The cutter can remove the tulle from even the smallest space and is versatile: It can be used as a sculpting tool for rounding out the body of a snowman, for creating more dimension on a straw hat, to remove excess stitches, and to eliminate wayward thread tails on the thread appliqué surface—a touch of the tip and the tail disappears.

and stop again. Believe me, all this stopping and starting would drive you nuts! Another down side is that on the back of the quilt there would be a silhouette where there is no quilting. Also, larger thread appliqués add a lot of weight and stiffness to the quilt, making it more difficult to maneuver under the head of the sewing machine.

That said, there are times the thread appliqué must be inserted between seams as the background is appliquéd together. Look at the grass along the river's edge in Figure 5-7. Adding the grass into the seams rather than thread painting it directly to the quilt top gives added dimension to the top. Also, sometimes a tree's upper branches and trunk are stitched to the quilt top before quilting in order for the canopy to thread paint over it.

To attach thread appliqués:

❶ Audition all of the thread appliqués on the quilt top, moving them around until you are pleased with their location. Stand back and be critical, as moving the thread appliqué even a fraction one way or another can make a huge difference in the visual appeal of the finished quilt.

❷ Place a small amount of water-soluble glue on the back of each thread appliqué and glue it in place. Glue works much better than pins, dries quickly, and washes away.

❸ Place polyester invisible thread on the upper spindle and whatever thread you used when you quilted the quilt in the bobbin.

❹ Set the zigzag stitch for 1–2mm and zigzag the thread appliqué in place. Use

Figure 5-6
LIFE IN HOLLY RIDGE, *detail. Full quilt on pages 6-7.*

Attaching the Thread Appliqué

The thread appliqué is not added to the quilt top until the borders, binding, label, and quilting are completed. There is a good reason for this. Let's assume that the people, wagons, and horses were added before the quilt was quilted (see figure 5-6). Every time you quilted up to one of the thread appliqués, you would have to stop and jump over the design and start again. You would get to the next thread appliqué and you'd have to start a light stitch by inserting one stitch in the fabric and one in the thread appliqué. You need just enough stitches to securely hold the appliqué in place, not a heavy satin stitch. Zigzag around the appliqué.

DIRECT METHOD

In the Direct method of thread painting the design is stitched directly onto the quilt top or fabric. Designs selected for the Direct method should have a low- to medium-stitch density, which results in light and airy designs, or small designs where the outside edges are too fragile or small to cut out.

The Direct method consists of two pieces of water-soluble stabilizer backing on the bottom; the fabric or quilt top in the middle; and a layer of water-soluble stabilizer film on top onto which the design is drawn. Follow steps 1–14 on page 37 for Tracing and Hooping the Design.

Removing the Stabilizer

1 Cut away the stabilizer from the front and back as close to the design as possible.

2 Follow the directions in steps 1–6 under Removing the Stabilizer on page 38.

3 Steam press any wrinkles from the back of the quilt top. Avoid direct iron contact with the thread as the sheen on some threads will turn dull if the iron touches them.

Larger, more complex designs should always follow the Direct method instructions above but small, simple designs can be traced right onto the background fabric. Simply tape the master pattern to a light box, tape the background fabric on top, and lightly trace the design onto the fabric with a mechanical pencil or marker. The pencil lines will be covered up during thread painting. Some of the small circle quilts in chapter 10 follow this method.

CONCLUSION

Designs using the Tulle Sandwich method not only sit above the surface of the quilt top but they also create dimension and give the illusion of something being closer to you. Designs thread painted directly to the fabric or quilt top sink into the fabric, giving the illusion of distance. Small designs that have a solid outside edge and can be cut out should be considered for the Tulle Sandwich method.

For example, look at figure 5-7. By using the Tulle Sandwich method, the fishing float appears to really be floating on the water. Had it been thread painted directly to the fabric, the threads would have sunk into the fabric and there would be no realism to the float. The same holds true of the small worms escaping from the can (see figure 5-8). They give the illusion that they are actually wriggling on the surface. The lesson here is to choose the best thread-painting method to meet a specific design's requirements.

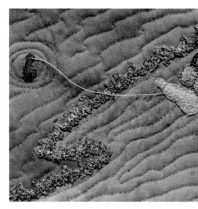

Figure 5-7
GOIN' FISHIN' *grass and fishing float*

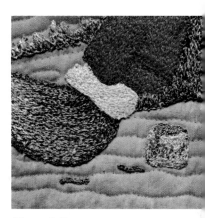

Figure 5-8
GOIN' FISHIN' *worms*

Tip: *In small quilts you might want to glue all the thread appliqués down at once, but in larger quilts where stiffness and weight can make a difference, glue them down and attach them one at a time.*

6

Shading, Blending, *and* Highlighting

After reading this chapter you will see you don't have to be an art major to create realistic thread-painted designs with shading, blending, and highlighting. Just a few basic art tips, a little common sense, and this simple rule will do the trick: thread paint the design the way it grows or exists in nature and the result will be realistic.

LIGHT AND SHADOW

Understanding this is easy if you know a little about light and shadows. Light gives a feeling that a part of an object is closer; shadows give a feeling of depth. Both help to give the illusion of three dimensions in a one-dimension object.

The idea with shading is to be subtle. It is better to under shade than over shade and poor shading is worse than no shading at all. Not only does shading create depth and form but it also can add rounding to a design such as on cheekbones, pumpkins, or the body of a snowman—basically anything circular. Shading is a versatile little fellow!

Remember: A dark area of the design tells the eye there is depth and distance. Light tells the eye that something is raised or closer to you. If you want the design to appear flat, it needs to have the same color throughout. When it comes to highlights, really make them bright or light. The more contrast, the more life is given to the design.

Without light and shadow, even the most perfectly executed thread-painted design is going to look flat. Shadows fool the viewer into seeing depth that is not there. The light source on an object and the shadow the light creates is what defines its shape.

Shadows are everywhere every day, but normally we don't try and figure out where the light is coming from or how many light sources there are or what the quality of the light is like. How the shadows are thread painted will tell all that to the viewer.

If the shadow is thread painted in the wrong place, the viewer will know something is wrong, but won't know why. But we are getting ahead of ourselves. Before we can determine where the highlights and shading go, we must determine the location of the light source.

LOCATING THE LIGHT SOURCE

The light source should be the same for the entire project. If the light source is to the design's right, then the right side will be in highlight and the left side in shadow. Also, any area within the design blocked by the light source will appear in shadow. For example, a fold in a lady's dress will cast a shadow behind the fold.

Some of the most obvious places to look for shadows in a design include:

– – – **People:** Look at the base of the hair; at the bend of the arm where the arm meets the body; underneath hats; where legs bend or come together; where fabric is folded.

– – – **Animals:** Look at the turn of the head; it might block an area below the head. Check the bend of a leg, the belly, or the area under the neck.

– – – **Trees, shrubs and other landscape elements:** Look to the side of the tree or shrub away from the light source, where the shrubs or trees

Figure 6-1
LIFE IN HOLLY RIDGE

Figure 6-2
LIFE IN HOLLY RIDGE
wagon

touch or get close to the ground. Look where rocks come together or touch the ground, or where a shrub or tree is being blocked by a landscape element in front of it.

These are just a few examples. Go outside on a sunny day at different times of the day, see how the shadows move around, and pay attention to the location of the sun.

The season of the year can also affect the direction of the light source. Check magazines, copyright-free Internet images, travel pamphlets, and photographs and really scrutinize the photos and images to familiarize yourself with how light and shadows affect each design in spring, summer, autumn, and winter.

Let's look at a couple of examples to see how shadows and light affect a design. In *LIFE IN HOLLY RIDGE* (Figure 6-1), I assumed that the sun was to the top left of the quilt. Any highlights throughout the designs would be on the left side. Any shadows would be to the right.

More complicated designs require a little more scrutiny. Look at the large wagon in figure 6-2. Keeping the scenario as above, the most light would reflect off the left side of the wagon, which is out of sight. However, the rear of the wagon is closer to the sun's source, so naturally it appears lighter than the right side of the wagon, which is in more shadow. The left front and rear wheels are the darkest wheels because they are in complete shade under the wagon, whereas the right front and rear wheels are lighter, because although the light source comes from the left, with the wagon positioned as it is, there is more light on the wheels on that side.

The idea here is to scrutinize the design before selecting the thread. Make mental notes where the light and shadows go. If necessary, trace the design on paper and use colored pencils to audition colors. Putting a little homework into the design first makes the transition from idea to actual thread painting much easier and less open for mistakes along the way.

In some ways it is easier to shade and highlight with thread than mixing paints on a pallet. There are more shades of thread to choose from than there are paints, and the best part is no mixing is required to get the right color. Your eye does all the mixing for you. How cool is that?

THREAD SELECTION

So what are the determining factors in selecting the thread colors for each design? Do you choose the shading color first, the blending color first, or the highlight color first? Well, it depends. Thread selection depends on the design element to be thread painted.

- – – **Trees and shrubs** I start with the shading color, which is the darkest green or seasonal color first, then move on to the blending colors, which act as a buffer between the darkest and lightest thread color. Finally, I apply the highlight color. This scenario assumes that the light source is either in front of or to the side of the tree or shrub. The entire foliage of the tree would be

*Figure 6-3
Orchid tree*

in light if the sun is in front of the tree. Having the sun to one side of the tree gives a little more creative license. Let's assume the light is coming from the right, as in figure 6-3. Obviously, the right side of the canopy would be in highlight, but from here let your creative urges flow. Hopscotch some highlights on the opposite side of the tree in selected areas to suggest a hint of light (see the hopscotch stitch on page 34). This is the place to have some fun and let the artist within you shine.

- – – **People's clothing and hair** For clothing and hair I start with the blending colors first, add the shading, and apply the highlight colors last. It is easier to select the blending colors first because I have a good idea of the core color I want for each element of clothing or hair. From there I choose the shading color, determine the degree of shadow, and finally decide what the highlight will be.

*Figure 6-4
Dog*

– – – **Animals** Animals are one of my most favorite elements to thread paint because of their variety. Some are solid, some have a calico or palomino look, and the color choices are endless. I work with a photograph or I have researched it online and have a good idea of the colors for that particular animal. For solid-colored animals, I start with the blending, then shading, and add the highlights last. For multi-colored animals I do the same, choosing the body color before the shading and highlighting colors.

The shading color can be used to define one part from another such as in figure 6-4, where the shading around the dog's legs help to define them from the body. On the darker parts of the body, scrutinize each part; most will start with the blending color and be accented with the shading and highlight colors. Animals are fantastic because they have "parts" going in all directions, which make for some interesting thread effects and color combinations.

– – – **Inanimate objects** Everything from wagons, carts, rocks, wheelbarrows, and fruit stands all have their own idiosyncrasies that need special attention depending on their location in the design. For example, refer to the wagon in figure 6-1 on page 44. For the main body of the wagon I started with the blending color, then added the shading and highlight colors. However, in selecting the left front and rear wheels, I started with the shading colors first because it was more critical to give the illusion of almost complete shadow to give the design the realism it needed.

Once the shading colors were selected, it was simple to choose a few complementary blending colors. Because the wheels were in complete shadow, there were no highlight colors.

The bottom line here is to determine the most critical color choices first and then shade, blend, or highlight from there. Each design has its own personality, so let the design talk to you. Believe me, it has a lot to say.

DETERMINING THE COLOR FAMILY

A good place to start when selecting threads is to choose threads within the same color family. A color family contains the same hue or tint throughout. For example, green threads can have a blue, gray, or olive cast to them. Blue threads can have a purple, green, or gray cast. Red threads can have a purple, orange, or gray cast. Choosing the correct blending, shading, and highlighting colors within the color family are important to give the design realism. Select blending colors to do just that—blend, not stand out in a crowd. The shading or highlighting colors will take care of getting all the attention.

It may be necessary to travel to other color families to get just the right emphasis needed for a particular design. It is easier at first to stay within the same color family, but don't get so caught up that you ignore a much better possibility in another family. Don't be afraid to branch out and experiment with unexpected shading and highlighting colors.

CHOOSING SHADING THREADS

Realistic shading requires gradual blending of dark, medium, and light threads. When I started experimenting with shading, my assumption was to use black or gray to shade and white to highlight. I found out very quickly that these colors are too stark and strong for most designs. While the shading and highlighting needs to be visible, you don't want it to be overpowering. Instead of a black or gray, use a darker shade of the major color family.

For example, look at the farmer in figure 6-5. A dark brown taupe within the taupe color family was used for shading the vest and under his arm, a dark blue for shading the pants, gray for shading the shirt, and a dark gold to shade the back of his hat. The shading and highlighting have been incorporated into the design correctly to give it depth, form, and dimension. These in turn give the design its realism.

In contrast to the correctly shaded farmer, notice the lack of shading and highlighting in the figure 6-6 farmer. He appears flat with no shape or depth. Most importantly, he is completely devoid of interest and realism.

In figure 6-7 the shading in the lady's hair depicts a darker tone where it is pulled

Figure 6-5
Farmer with
shading

Figure 6-6
Farmer with
no shading

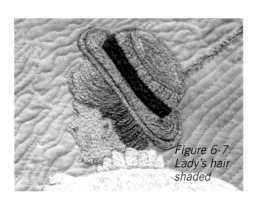

Figure 6-7
Lady's hair
shaded

Figure 6-8
Green apples

away from her neck, plus her head is turning, which puts the back of her hair in a slight shadow. So don't leave the shading and highlighting out—it is what gives realism to each design.

Complementary colors also work well to add shading to the design. They are directly opposite each other on the color wheel and are based on differences rather than similarities and they make each color appear brighter. In figure 6-8 a dark shade of green was used to shade the apple on the left and the complementary color red was used as a shading color. Does the apple on the right appear brighter?

Be aware that some thread families may not have a color strong enough to act as a shading color. White may need a medium gray or taupe as a shading color; yellow might need a gray or gold or taupe. Making samples makes the selection process easier.

CHOOSING BLENDING THREADS

Blending is the placing of two colors next to each other in such a way that they are perceived to be mixed, even though they are not. Blending colors are the core colors of the design; generally, there isn't a big jump in value between colors. They should complement each other as these colors will be the ones most prevalent in the design.

The size of the design will determine the number of blending colors. One color would be appropriate for a very small design, up to 4 or more for larger designs. It is easiest to choose blending colors to begin with that are your favorite colors. Favorites are a great place to start, but give your imagination a whirl as you progress and step out of the box and try some colors you are not as comfortable with. You will be surprised at what you see.

To select blending colors, let's look at an example. Looking at figure 6-9, most people new to thread painting would choose threads 1-7 in order, beginning with the left-most thread. The problem is that threads 2 and 3 (from the left) will stitch out as the same color, as will 3 and 4.

Blending colors need to be at least two shades apart, and, depending on the color family, sometimes three or even four. The colors need to have enough value steps between them so you can tell one color from another but not be so bold that one stands out more than the other. Given the threads in figure 6-9, thread 1 is the shading color; threads 2 and 4 are the blending colors, and threads 6 or 7 are the highlights. There are enough differences between the two blending colors so that the threads will stitch in harmoniously but not compete with each other. Practice makes it much easier to choose the right threads automatically. Over time your eye will develop the ability to choose the right threads the first time. Of course, samples still must be made, but with practice, less time will be spent choosing blending threads.

CHOOSING HIGHLIGHT THREADS

Highlights occur where light hits an object, are usually quite small, and appear to be the closest part of the design to you. They add the spark, the bounce, and the light to a design and show the direction of the light source. Highlights normally are the lightest value in the color family, such as pink for a red family and coral for orange. Some families such as white do not have an apparent highlight. Try using a pale yellow, pale gray, cream, or pale blue as the highlight for white. Also, try selecting a highlight from the next color on the color wheel, such as a pale orange with cranberry, moss green with yellow, and aqua with dark green— just to get you started. Grab a hoop and a color wheel and experiment playing with highlight colors.

CREATING DEPTH WITH THREAD SELECTION AND STITCH WIDTH

Creating depth and distance with thread occurs in several ways; the easiest is with color. Remember that dark colors recede and light colors come forward.

Figure 6-9
Spools of thread

Figure 6-10
Illusion of depth

Figure 6-11
Horse

Another way to manipulate depth and distance is to choose a small zigzag width. Look at figure 6-10 and pages 24-25 and notice the dark green underside of the tree's canopy. First, a dark green thread was chosen to give the illusion of depth. Then, to help further emphasize depth, a small 2.0mm zigzag width was selected. The smallness of the stitch combined with the dark thread gives the illusion of depth and distance to the canopy. To give the illusion that the top part of the canopy is closer to the viewer, a lighter thread, which brings the design toward you, and a wider 4.5mm zigzag stitch were used. To give the final depth to the canopy, a dark green thread was hopscotched around the canopy in an irregular movement. This added shading draws the viewer's eye into the design.

UNEXPECTED COLOR

Try an unexpected thread color to add more punch to the design. Unexpected colors, even though not always necessarily readily visible to the eye, add depth and realism. These colors can be subtle or cry out for attention. Try a dark brown as the first thread-painted color on the branches of an evergreen tree. Then thread paint a dark green lightly over the brown. The dark brown literally draws the eye into the tree.

Another trick is to use yellow, dark blue, or taupe as the first color in grass. Around the bottom outside edge of a yellow center on a flower, try a medium orange as an accent. These colors, even though used in small amounts, make the design really jump off the fabric. The idea here is to use a subtle color to draw the eye in and a bright color to help draw attention to the design.

As mentioned earlier, thread cannot be mixed like paint so the eye needs to do all the mixing. How well the eye makes the mix is up to you. Haphazardly thread painting a color here and there with no idea of the final result is like building a bridge with no blueprints. The unexpected color is there for support and is not the leading character. For example, in figure 6-11 the horse would appear to be only black. But upon closer examination you find dark rust, navy blue, dark olive, and three shades of black. These unexpected colors not only give life and excitement and draw the eye into the horse, but they also kept me from being bored to death thread painting only one color.

THREAD SKETCHING

During the years I have taught thread painting, many students have asked for a design they could complete in a few hours. I decided to experiment to see what I could come up with. Rather than completely filling in the designs like I normally do in thread painting, I decided to just sketch a landscape. To my surprise, not only was the landscape completed in a short period of time, but it was also entirely realistic. And best of all, it was simple to do.

In my version of thread sketching, thread becomes the medium that gives the landscape the color, features, and excitement while the sketch created by the thread is something that is light and airy with little definition—close to realistic but with a hint of detail. Thread sketching is meant to give the idea of a simple landscape or design but isn't intended to capture its entire essence (see figure 7-1; see chapter 10 for project information).

As in thread painting, the only stitches used to thread sketch are a straight and zigzag stitch. Because the biggest

Figure 7-1
Completed
thread sketch

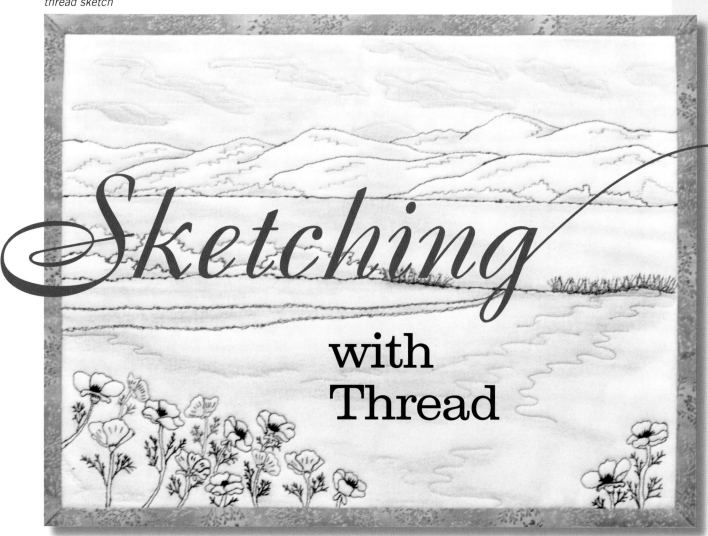

Figure 7-2
Funky flower fabric

Tip: *When using any loosely woven fabric, fuse a piece of lightweight stabilizer or woven interfacing to the back of the fabric to give stability to the stitches once the water-soluble stabilizer backing is washed away.*

percentage of the landscape is a line drawing, a straight stitch is used most often. The zigzag stitch comes into play when more definition and more stitching are required within a specific area of the project. Tsukineko inks, colored pencils, and oil-based colored pencils add the final touch to bring your thread-sketched landscape or design to life.

As in the Direct method of thread painting, the design is traced onto a piece of water-soluble stabilizer, the fabric is stabilized, then hooped, and you are ready to sketch (see page 37 for detailed instructions). What you have already learned about the different types of thread-painting stitches, hooping the design, and cleaning up the design in chapter 5 applies to thread sketching as well—just in a lighter format.

The selection of fabrics is endless. You can use a white, cream, or color Kona cotton or any type of commercial fabric to sketch onto such as quilting fabric, canvas, twill, silk, denim, linen, and anything else that might appeal to you. Play around with fun fabrics like canvas to see what happens. The extra dimension might be just what you are looking for in your next project. In fact, thread sketching on canvas gives the look of a painting from a distance.

The thread type and weight selection is the same as in thread painting (see chapter 2 for detailed information). Use a solid color 40-weight thread for the line drawings and a 40-weight variegated thread for tree canopies, small shrub groupings, and to depict water movement in meandering streams and rivers. Metallic thread shows its luster on moon-crested snow scenes. Use 60- or 100-weight threads in small confined areas or small parts of the design requiring more detail.

Most thread-sketching designs are light and airy, so distortion is not a factor. A single layer of water-soluble stabilizer backing is all that is necessary to support the fabric from underneath. Use 2 layers of stabilizer if the design calls for a higher stitch density. Clear water-soluble stabilizer film is used to trace the design.

Don't forget to fuse interfacing to the back of loosely woven fabrics. The hoop selection is the same as in thread painting, although a spring or plastic hoop can be used since distortion is not an issue. I still recommend the screw hoop for all designs simply because the tension can be controlled inside the hoop.

While the projects in this book are landscapes, any design you can create with

Redwork can be thread sketched just by changing the colors of the thread in the design. Try using shades of black to gray or flesh to taupe to create a portrait of your child or grandchild. Animals can be portrayed in monochromatic or life-like colors. And how about using some bright neon colors to add some thread-sketched animals to a child's first quilt? Ideas build on ideas, so let your creativity shine and I think you will be surprised where it leads.

How about printing a photograph or design from a graphics program such as Adobe® Photoshop® or Adobe® Photoshop® Elements software and enhancing the photo using thread sketching? The beauty here is that there are no copyright issues involved with your own photographs and designs. The printed fabric automatically gives you the lines to thread sketch, and since there is a printed surface underneath the thread, it isn't necessary to fill in the entire design.

A thread-sketching project can be simple or complex. That is your call, and it is a fun way to become comfortable playing with thread.

Whether thread painting or thread sketching, I don't think you will ever look at nature quite the same way again. It is amazing what we miss because we simply don't see what is before us. Thread painting and sketching teaches you to look for the detail needed to give realism to the design, thus creating a better trained eye for what exists around us.

THREAD SKETCHING ON COMMERCIAL FABRIC

Walk into any fabric or quilt shop and your senses will be overwhelmed with all the beautiful fabric for your selection.

One day while browsing at my favorite quilt shop, a particularly intriguing piece of fabric caught my eye. I had no idea what I was going to do with it when I got it home, but of course I bought it any way. A few weeks later I dug it out, stared at it for a bit, found a funky flower within the fabric and decided to try a little creative stitching. Thread sketching was new to me at the time and I thought it would fit the bill nicely.

A few hours later I had a completed project! What fun and so quick! Best of all, I didn't have to come up with a design or figure out the thread colors because the flowers did all the talking and choosing for me. The newly added threads totally brought the project to life. Figure 7-2 on page 52 shows a section of the fabric. Figure 7-3 shows an upclose section of one of the flowers that was thread sketched. Notice that all of the areas of

Figure 7-3
FUNKY FLOWER
up close

Figure 7-4
FUNKY FLOWER
complete

Right, top to bottom:

Figure 7-5
Black-and-white-
fabric

Figure 7-6
Thread painted
black-and-white
fabric

the flower were not sketched and some of the background left as it was. Figure 7-4 shows a photo of the completed quilt.

Thread painting being my first love and not willing to leave the status quo alone, I scrounged around and found a nifty little black-and-white commercial fabric perfect to thread paint. Figure 7-5 shows a sample section of the fabric, figure 7-6 the completed quilt top. All I did was figure out the section of the fabric I liked and thread painted away. The lines in the leaves and cherries gave me a good idea where to highlight and shade. This project took me a bit longer than sketching to complete but I loved the results just the same.

One of the other plusses to thread sketching on commercial fabric or your own custom-printed background fabric is that not all areas need to be completely filled in with thread. The color is already there, so use it to your advantage. Thread sketch some of the design lightly and leave other areas with just the background showing. The combination of the two methods actually makes the thread-sketched areas shine even more.

To get started, support the fabric with two pieces of water-soluble stabilizer backing and hoop the design. No top stabilizer is needed because the design is already on the fabric. Once the design is complete, fuse a piece of fusible web to the back, cut out the design with very sharp scissors, and fuse it to your quilted top. Depending on the fabric, you might want to use a little thread sealant and a paint brush and seal the edges, especially if the fabric is loosely woven. Zigzag around the edges lightly with invisible polyester thread if the finished project is to be handled.

*Figure 8-1
Distortion monster*

There is a little distortion monster that is waiting to wreak havoc with high-stitch density thread-painted designs (see figure 8-1). Low-density designs such as small shrubs or light and airy fall tree canopies are not a distortion issue. But high-density designs such as large tree trunks and snowmen consist of a lot of stitches in a confined space, and the distortion monster likes to rear its ugly head in these larger designs.

The Distortion Monster

SHRINKAGE AND DISTORTION

Distortion can never be eliminated even when the design is properly hooped and stabilized. So it is up to you to select the proper thread-painting method to minimize the damage distortion can do (see chapter 5). In addition it is imperative that the proper hoop, hoop size, and the correct stabilizer are selected (see chapter 3).

One of the biggest distortion makers is the zigzag stitch. There is air space between the zig and zag and every time the machine completes the stitch, there is a pull on the fabric or stabilizer. This constant pulling causes the fabric or stabilizer to shrink in the direction of the stitches and stretch in the opposite direction. Wider zigzag stitches create more distortion than their narrower counterparts.

As a rule of thumb, if you can create a design as a stand-alone thread appliqué, use the Tulle Sandwich method—this means the outside edges are solid (see page 37). This way any distortion is pushed to the outside edges of the stabilizer and is easily cut away. Distortion can form around the outside edges of designs in the Direct method as well, but normally these small ripples can be quilted out (see page 41).

Shrinkage occurs normally with medium- to high-stitch density designs. To deal with shrinkage, enlarge designs to assure the proper finished size. For example, let's assume you are thread painting a boy whose drawn size is approximately 6". Enlarge the design 105 percent to allow for shrinkage so the finished thread-painted boy will end up being 6" tall. I wish I had a magic formula to give you

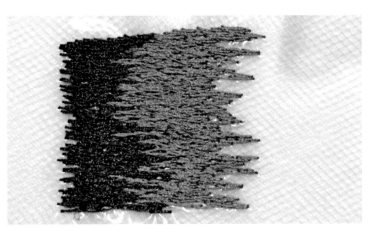

*Figure 8-2
Zigzag, 1st
color samples*

*Figure 8-3
Zigzag, 2nd
color samples*

to determine the percentage of enlargement, but the amount of shrinkage is
due to the size of the design, whether a
straight or zigzag stitch is used, the size
and type of hoop, and the type of stabilization used. An enlargement of 5–10
percent will work for most designs, and
with experience you will more easily be
able to determine the proper amount.

SAMPLES

Successful thread painting depends on
the selection of correct thread colors.
Proper selection of shading, highlighting,
and blending colors makes all the difference between a realistic design and one

that creates havoc with the eye. Making
samples allows me the opportunity to
choose my thread colors, and most importantly, to do a practice run on designs
I haven't attempted before.

To assure success, audition the thread
colors by first making samples using either stabilizer film or the same fabric and
stabilizer in a practice hoop. To begin,
set the zigzag stitch to 4.5 and move the
hoop east to west, thread painting the
lines of color fairly close together and
leaving the edges jagged as shown in
figure 8-2.

Take the second thread color and thread
paint into the stitches already in place,
again making the outside edges jagged
(see figure 8-3). Continue thread painting and substituting threads until all of
the anticipated colors are auditioned (see
figure 8-4).

This exercise may take a few minutes
or a few hours but it is important that all
colors are selected before beginning the
final design. Now this doesn't mean that
you can't change your mind as to color
choices as the design progresses, but it
gives you a definite starting point that you
know will be realistic.

*Figure 8-4
Zigzag, com-
plete samples*

On other simple designs like the snow-man shown in figure 8-5, I partially thread painted all areas of the design to make sure my colors were correct. On the trees in the same project I wasn't sure which colors would look right with white snow, so I made samples of several different colors. It was easy once I made the samples; visually, the lighter birch-like colors worked best with a snow scene (see figure 8-6).

On more complicated designs, make a sample of the area that is a concern for you. For example, the dog's head in figure 8-7 was a bit scary for me because I had not done anything like that be-fore. I wasn't sure of the thread weights and colors around the dog's mouth and around his nose. So I made a sample of the dog's head to assure the final design would be the way I wanted it. It took a couple of times playing around with dif-ferent threads and weights to get it right, and the practice gave me the confidence to move forward. A sample of the whole design isn't necessary, just the area, or part of an area, will work.

THREAD JOURNAL

Once the colors are selected, I write in a thread journal the thread manufacturer, color, thread weight, the stitch selection, and if using a zigzag stitch, what width is required. As I progress with the design, I may make minor changes to the stitch width or I may have specific comments about problems with the design. Accurate record keeping is important so at a later date I can refer to the colors for a similar design. Over time you will develop a core grouping of threads that you use over and over again because you know they work. While I think I will remember the exact colors, I find that by the next day (or even

Figure 8-5
Snowman

Figure 8-6
Trees

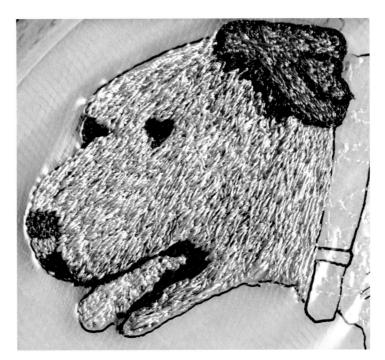

Figure 8-7
Sample of dog head

a few hours later) the thread numbers have completely disappeared from my mind. Keep an accurate journal—you will be surprised how many times you refer to it.

Thread Painting with Style NANCY PRINCE

The quilt is quilted, the thread appliqués have been attached, the quilt has been blocked, the binding is on, and it's ready to hang on the wall. There is one more step that needs to be done to give the quilt the final realism it needs.

SHADOWS CAST BY THREAD-PAINTED DESIGNS

In Chapter 6 we discovered the importance of shading within the thread appliqué to create realism. Landscape quilts have a secondary shading area as well—the shadow cast by the completed thread appliqué onto the quilt surface. This shadow is an integral part and major contributing factor to creating realism and depth throughout the entire quilt. In thread painting, leaving the shadow out would be like leaving the baking powder out of a cake—it would be flat and unappealing.

The *Final* Touches

Figure 10-1
LIFE IN HOLLY
RIDGE *with*
no shading

Figure 10-1 shows *LIFE IN HOLLY RIDGE* without any shadows under the thread appliqués. The quilt has the appearance of being completely flat, with little warmth. It lacks interest, not to mention that you feel like something is missing. In figure 10-2 the shadows have been added under the wagons, animals, and people throughout the town. Just the addition of the shadows totally changes the look and feel of the quilt. The quilt has warmth, realism, and gives the feeling the viewer can walk right into the quilt. Adding the shadows made the thread appliqués literally pop off the quilt. As a side benefit, the shadows help accentuate the thread appliqués. Don't leave this

step out. It may be scary at first, but it is so worth the final results. Just don't forget to practice first.

DETERMINING THE LOCATION OF THE SHADOWS

The sun rises in the east and sets in the west. In the early morning as the sun rises overhead, the shadows are long and form to the west of the object. At noon, the shadows are short and northerly. As the sun sets in the west, the shadows cast from the designs are long and form to the east.

So how do you decide where the shadows go? Starting with a personal photograph or picture is a good place to begin since the light and shadows have been decided for you. Or, look at the landscape and the designs you have in mind and choose one of the light scenarios on the preceeding page to decide on the location of the sun based on where you want the shadows to fall. If you are an artist and can paint the shadows onto the quilt top before it is quilted, terrific. See chapter 6 for more on light and shadows.

As for me, I never know exactly where the thread appliqués are going to go until they are stitched to the quilt top after quilting. The shadows are not added until the quilt top is done, and that includes the binding.

To create the shadows cast by the appliqués on the fabric, I use Tuskineko inks. These bottles of ink or ink pads are very user-friendly and come in a variety of colors. The teammate to go along with the ink pads are Fantastix brushes. They come in rounded and pointed versions; for shading use the pointed Fantistix. The ink pads are easier to work with but are not permanent, so stick with the bottles of ink if washing the quilt is a possibility.

Figure 10-2 LIFE IN HOLLY RIDGE *with shading*

Small quilts are best inked on a flat surface, but for larger quilts I normally hang the quilt on the wall to give me a better perspective so that I can stand back from time to time to critique my progress.

Now, I must admit that taking ink to a completed quilt is a bit terrifying. Hundreds and sometimes thousands of hours have been spent completing this little masterpiece and an "Oops!" at this point would be a disaster. To avoid a major mistake, practice for at least thirty minutes on a sample piece of the same makeup as the quilt top fabric. This will "pattern" your hand so you will know how much ink to rub off before starting and how firm the pressure on the brush needs to be. Once your confidence has built up on the practice piece, you will be ready to start on the quilt top.

Start slowly, proceed with caution, and take your time. I start shading underneath the simplest thread appliqué and apply the ink in layers. The first layer lightly defines where I think the edges of the shadow should be. This way if a mistake is made, it is much easier to blend these light shadows into the quilt top. To begin, pour a small amount of Cool Gray Tsukineko ink into a small container. Dip the point into the ink and with the brush on its side—you will be shading with the side of the brush and not the point—rub off the majority of the ink on all sides of the brush. The brush will be almost completely dry to begin shading.

Go slowly and stand back and critique the quilt from a distance from time to time, as it is easy to lose your perspective up close. Evaluate the shadows and have a buddy look at the shading for their opinion, too. Once the shadows look realistic, darken the images with other layers of ink until the desired degree of darkness is achieved. If the shading from the ink doesn't get down into the quilting lines, use the dry tip on the brush to add the shading to the valley where the quilting lines are. Remember: The brush should be practically dry. The idea here is to rub off most of the ink before touching the quilt top. A blob of black ink on your perfectly finished quilt top cannot be removed.

Even though it appears that shadows are the gospel, there will be times when no or relatively few shadows are called for. For example, on cloudy or snowy days or at high noon, the shadows would be small and northerly or directly underneath the design. A $1/4"-1/2"$ shader paint brush (the bristles on the brush are at a 45-degree angle) or a $1/4"$ fabric painting brush (these bristles are very stiff) can be used in place of Fantastix brushes to get the ink into the quilting lines.

As a side note, Tsukineko inks can be used to shade and ink areas on a traditional appliqué quilt or to enhance the background fabric. I use the ink to shade areas on my commercially available printed background to enhance an area and give it more depth. These inks work perfectly to shade or increase the shade on flower petals, leaves and stems, or any object that would benefit from a darker image. Lighter inks can be used to highlight as well. Tsukineko inks are versatile little fellows and there are way more creative ways to use them, so see what your inquisitive mind can come up with.

EMBELLISHING THE QUILT

Embellishing your quilt as you progress or when it is done is just way too much fun. One idea leads to another and all of a sudden all sorts of unexpected avenues open up.

To encourage creativity, stroll down any aisle at a craft store. Craft stores offer an enormous wealth of embellishments for your quilt. Sometimes a little creative license is needed but all you have to do is spend some time browsing the aisles and you will be amazed how easily even the simplest embellishment can be modified to suit your needs. For example:

– – – **Fimo® clay** This user-friendly clay comes in an assortment of colors and can be used to make small buttons for clothing, belt buckles, dog tags, harness rings for horses, small signs, small flowers, and stems—the list is endless. Pop the item into the oven for a few minutes and the clay is hardened and ready to use. Use multiple colors of Fimo in one design for even more fun. Because the final image is hard, use this only on wall quilts.

– – – **Bias tape** Oh, the fun I have had with bias tape! In figure 10-2 on page 61, all the buildings were constructed using the folded edges of bias tape. Half-inch pieces of bias tape were fused to interfacing and constructed just like building a wood-sided house. The doors and windows were painted on prepared-for-dying fabric, cut out, and then fused on the buildings. The layering of the bias tape gives the finished buildings and houses more dimension and the feeling that someone actually lives in them. Bias tape also comes in a very small check pattern that can be used to augment people's clothing, baskets of food, etc.

– – – **Rickrack or small ribbon** Use small rickrack or ribbon to decorate people's clothing.

– – – **Decorative buttons** It seems there is a button for every use. In *Life in Holly Ridge* (see figure 10-1) there was a tiny fish at the end of a fishing pole, and I didn't want to have to thread paint the detail in something so small. So I searched craft stores until I found a button that looked like a fish. There are buttons that are flowers, children's toys, teddy bears—the list is endless and effective.

– – – **Check out the jewelry department** I could browse this aisle forever. Use the clear, flexible, plastic-covered wire for fishing lines, the suede for horse reins, small clasps for bridle and harness apparel for horses, beads, shells, and all things sparkly for just about anything.

– – – **Flannel or lightweight batting** Place a piece of flannel or thin batting under houses, buildings, or bridges to raise the design from the surface of the quilt. This gives the design more dimension, causing it to come forward.

– – – **Stuffing** To give a 3-D look to your designs, try stuffing them. In figure 10-3 the boy sitting on the fence posed a problem when the design was complete. In order for the fence to run straight, the boy was too large for the area. I could have forced him to fit the space, but I decided to stuff him instead. The 3-D look was just too cute!

These are just a few ideas for ways to embellish your quilt. Each quilt determines its own embellishment, so let the quilt talk to you to tell you what it needs for that extra spark. The attention to detail is what makes the quilt shine.

Figure 10-3
Boy on fence

The projects in the book are for you to enjoy making and to raise your comfort level so you can portray your own ideas in thread. Refer to chapter 4 for a refresher on the thread-painting stitches.

Thread charts with each project show the thread numbers, areas to thread paint, thread colors, stitch selection, and hoop movements. The section on preparing the Fusible Web Border Circle Templates on page 70 applies to all four circle quilts—SPRING'S MORNING, A SUMMER DAY, GOLDEN DAYS, and FIRST SNOWFALL. Read Assembling the Background before beginning a project.

The custom printed background fabric for the four circle quilts and SEARCHING FOR BUTTERFLIES can be purchased from my website (see Resources on page 127). If you want to piece the background fabric but not the small houses for the circle quilts, these can be purchased as well. Certain notions, fusing supplies, and appliqué steps can be omitted when purchasing my custom printed fabric; these will be noted with each set of instructions.

Directions also appear on my website for suggested quilting designs and ideas for each project. See Resources on page 127.

Thread Painting

Projects

SPRING'S MORNING

A SUMMER DAY

GOLDEN DAYS

FIRST SNOWFALL

ADDING MUSLIN STRIPS

❶ To diminish distortion, the background fabric and stabilizer must fit securely in the hoop. Sometimes the design to thread paint lies at the edge of the quilt top where there is not enough fabric to fit in the hoop properly. When this happens, cut a piece of muslin 2"–3" wide by the length of the sides, top, and bottom, and machine baste it along the edge of the quilt with a 1/4" seam allowance. Press the seam allowance toward the muslin strip. Sometimes only one edge is affected, sometimes all edges are affected. The stabilizer should fit underneath the muslin strips. Remove the muslin when the design is complete.

❷ Be careful to thread paint just to the edge of the muslin and do not catch the seam allowance in the thread work.

MATERIALS AND CUTTING FOR THE FOUR CIRCLE QUILTS

Fabric yardage assumes that fabric is 40" wide after shrinkage and that all 4 circle projects are made into one quilt that measures approximately 31" x 31".

Because thread painting will cause some distortion, please measure your project before cutting muslin, sashing, border, or binding strips. Measurements given here are approximations.

- – – 1 yard olive green tone-on-tone fabric for the borders, sashing, and binding

- – – 1 yard brown tone-on-tone for the inside and outside borders

- – – 1 fat quarter teal tone-on-tone for the inside borders

- – – Backing – 1 1/4 yards

- – – Batting – 37" x 37"

- – – Temporary spray adhesive

Tips for any thread-painting project

- – – Move the hoop slowly and with an even speed. Even when the pedal speed is very fast, continue moving the hoop with a slow, even speed.

- – – You don't need a death grip on the hoop— just a light touch to guide it around. Lightly rest your finger tips on the east and west edges of the hoop. Avoid holding the hoop on the south edge or the back of the hoop will rise up.

- – – Use the needle-down function on your machine to help secure the hoop before rotating.

- – – Make sure the outside edges of all Tulle Sandwich method designs are solid before washing out the stabilizer. Hold the design up to a light and any unfilled holes will become apparent. It is not necessary to fill in the pin prick holes, but any hole you can see with your naked eye should be filled. Holes left at the edge of the designs leave an unsightly hole when the stabilizer is washed away and the tulle removed.

- – – Keep the line you are thread painting parallel to you when using the zigzag stitch as a fill stitch.

- - - When using a muslin strip at the edge of the quilt top, make sure the stabilizer backing fits underneath the muslin.

- - - When working on a Tulle Sandwich design, any area outside the drawn design is free space in which to practice. If you are uncertain how the stitch will look, use these areas for practice; they will be cut away once the design is complete.

- - - The larger the surface area, the wider the zigzag width; the smaller the surface, the narrower the width. Any time you feel out of control when using the zigzag stitch, reduce the width.

- - - Underlay with invisible thread when there are interior design lines you need to key off of. Underlay with the first thread color when there are none.

- - - Sometimes tangled threads get caught under the hoop or in the throat plate. To release the threads necessitates cutting the tangle and usually results in a hole in the stabilizer and tulle. To repair this hole, cut a patch from the outer edge of the sandwich consisting of all four layers. Place the patch on the back side of the hole and pin in place from the top surface. Continue thread painting, removing the pins and trimming away the excess patch once the area is complete.

- - - To keep stress off the hooped design, remove it from the hoop at the end of the day and place it in a sealable plastic bag to keep it clean and the water-soluble stabilizer pliable.

- - - For most designs use a 40-weight polyester or rayon thread on the top and a 60-weight in the bobbin. The lighter weight bobbin thread helps keep the design from becoming bulky.

- - - Select a silver or medium gray 60-weight bobbin fill for most designs. However, if

your tension is correct and no pesky bobbin thread is poking its head to the top, any color 60-weight can be used. Caveat: Never use a black or dark bobbin under white or pastel colors; the dark thread will shadow through and cause a white design to appear gray.

- - - When filling in designs, it is okay to stitch over threads already in place.

- - - It isn't necessary to adjust the length on either the straight or zigzag stitch. The length is controlled by how fast or slow the hoop is moved or by the machine speed.

- - - Keep a second hoop prepared with the same fabric and stabilizer as the project you are working on to make samples and to test thread colors.

- - - To relax and improve your accuracy, try some test stitches before beginning. Hoop a piece of muslin and stabilizer backing and just go play. Practice moving the hoop in all directions to see what happens to the stitches based on the direction of the hoop. This will make you much more comfortable before you begin your project.

- - - It is not necessary to tack the last stitch unless you are in an area that only has a few stitches.

- - - Any time you are in a confined area or need more control, reduce the motor speed on your machine.

- - - Regardless of the method you choose, thread paint all elements of the design in the hoop before rehooping. It is easier to change the thread than to keep moving the hoop around on the fabric to follow a specific thread color.

- - - Thread paint straight lines first. Distortion from other areas of the design causes straight lines to become wavy.

Olive Green Tone-on-Tone

Square Inside Circle Border
　　4 squares 12" x 12"

Sashing
　　2 strips 1³/₄" x 13⁵/₈" (vertical
　　　　center)
　　1 strip 1³/₄" x 28" (horizontal
　　　　center)

Outside Border (mitered)
　　4 strips 1³/₄" x 37" (sides, top, and
　　　　bottom)

Binding (double-fold)
　　4 strips 2¹/₄" x 40"

Brown Tone-on-Tone

Inside Borders (mitered)
　　8 strips ³/₄" x 11³/₄" (sides)
　　8 strips ³/₄" x 12¹/₂" (top and
　　　　bottom)

Outside Border (mitered)
　　4 strips 1¹/₄" x 32¹/₂" (sides, top, and
　　　　bottom)

Teal Tone-on-Tone

Teal Inner Border (butted)
　　8 strips 1" x 12¹/₂" (sides)
　　8 strips 1" x 13⁵/₈" (top and bottom)

CONSTRUCTING THE QUILT TOP

Adding the Green Circle Borders

1 Thread paint the 4 circle quilts:
Spring's Morning, A Summer Day,
Golden Days, and First Snowfall
(see figure 10-1).

2 Follow the instructions on page 70 for
making the circle border.

3 Square up each circle border to
11³/₄" x 11³/₄" (see figure 10-2). (Remember: Your measurements may vary.)

Adding the Brown Inside Borders

1 Sew 1 inside brown border to the
side of each of the 4 green circle
borders. Press.

Figure 10-1
Complete the 4 thread painted quilt tops.
Spring's Morning *is pictured above.*

Figure 10-2
The green border circle complete. First
Snowfall *is pictured above.*

2 Sew 1 inside brown border to the top and bottom of each of the 4 green circle borders (see figure 10-3). Miter the corners. Press.

Adding the Teal Borders

1 Sew 1 teal border to the sides of each of the 4 brown inside borders. Press.

2 Sew 1 teal border to the top and bottom of each of the 4 brown inside borders (see figure 10-4). Press.

Sashing

1 Add one 1³/₄" x 13⁵/₈" piece of sashing to the center of two of the background squares; repeat for the second 2 squares (see figure 10-5). Press.

2 Add one 1³/₄" x 28" piece of sashing to the bottom of 1 of the pieces above. Press. Stitch the sashing to the remaining 2 background squares.

3 Measure and square up if necessary before adding the outside brown border and green border.

Stitching the Outside Brown Border to the Outside Green Border

1 Stitch the outside brown borders to the outside green border. Press.

2 Miter the corners. Trim the seams and press open.

3 Spray baste the backing fabric. Smooth out the batting onto the backing. Turn over and press. Spray baste the batting and smooth the quilt top on top.

4 Quilting instructions are with each project.

Figure 10-5
Stitch one center green sashing to two of the completed circle borders.

Figure 10-3
Inside brown borders stitched in place.Note: Quilting is shown above but your quilting will be done once batting and backing are in place.

Figure 10-4
Inside teal borders stitched in place.

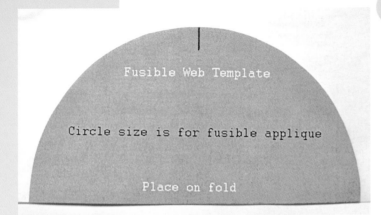

Fusible Web Template

Circle size is for fusible applique

Place on fold

Figure 1

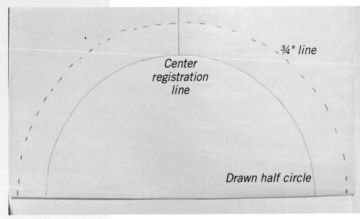

¾" line

Center registration line

Drawn half circle

Figure 2

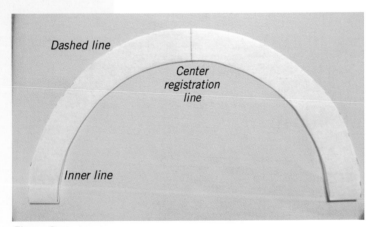

Dashed line

Center registration line

Inner line

Figure 3

Notions

- - - 1 piece of heavy paper such as card stock or poster board
- - - 4 pieces of 8½" x 8½" paper-backed fusible web
- - - Repositionable glue stick
- - - 4 pieces of 12" x 12" circle border fabric
- - - Spray starch

Preparing Fusible Templates

Note: Download the Free Fusible Web template at www.nancyprince.com/books

❶ Trace the template onto heavy paper.

❷ Cut out the half circle template.

❸ Using a repositionable glue stick, lightly glue the back of the template.

❹ Fold a piece of 8½" x 8½" fusible web in half with the fusible sides together.

❺ Position the cut-out template on the fold of the fusible web an equal distance from the right and left edges of the web (see figure 1).

❻ Trace around the template. Mark the registration line at the center of the half circle (see figure 2).

❼ Remove the template.

❽ Mark a dotted line ³/₄" from the outside edge of the drawn half circle line all the way around the perimeter (see figure 2). This cutting line does not have to be exact.

9 Cut out on the dashed outside line and the solid inner line (see figure 3).

10 Turn the web over and mark the center registration line on the other side of the web.

11 Open up the circle. Don't remove the paper backing until ready to fuse to fabric.

Preparing the Fabric Circle and Template

Note: Download the Free Fusible Web template at www.nancyprince.com

1 To make the border fabric easier to work with, spray the fabric heavily with spray starch. Press.

2 Take 1 of the 12" x 12" squares of border fabric for the circle and draw a line horizontally and vertically through the center on the wrong side of the fabric (see figure 4).

3 Match the vertical and horizontal registration lines on the fusible web with the drawn lines on the fabric, figure 4.

4 Fuse lightly in place according to manufacturer's directions, figure 4.

5 Fold with the right sides of the fabric together horizontally and finger press; the paper side of the fusible web is facing you.

6 Trace the fabric circle template onto heavy paper, cut out and lightly glue in place on the wrong side of the fabric, lining up the registration lines of the fabric circle template with the vertical line on the fabric, figure 5.

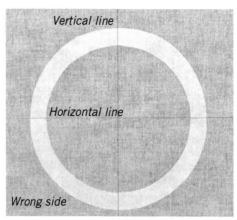

Figure 4

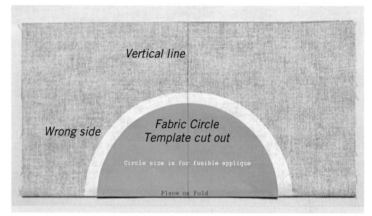

Figure 5

Tip: *Cut out a trial circle on a piece of muslin or scrap fabric first to make sure the circle fits. Thread painting causes the background fabric to shrink and the exact amount it will shrink is difficult to predict. It is not an issue if the circle is a bit too small, but the unfinished outside edge of the background fabric will show if the circle is too large. Adjust the final circle if necessary.*

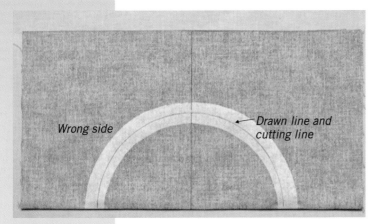

Wrong side

Drawn line and cutting line

Figure 6

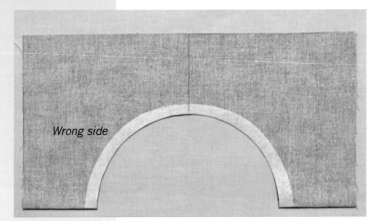

Wrong side

Figure 7

Figure 8

7 Trace around the outside of the template. Note the drawn line and cutting line in figure 6.

8 Carefully cut out on the inside drawn line. The arrow in figure 6 points to the cutting line. Remember, this is going to be fusible appliqué, so the edge needs to be a clean cut (see figure 7).

9 Don't remove the paper backing until you are ready to fuse, as the cut edge tends to fray if handled too much.

10 When ready, open up the fabric circle and audition the circle over the background fabric to make sure that it fits the way you want. It is better for the background circle to be a little too small than too big.

11 Cut away the excess background fabric from the quilt top circle leaving at least ½" of fabric.

12 Remove the paper backing from the fusible web and fuse in place following the manufacturer's directions (see figure 8).

13 Change to an open-toe appliqué foot and raise the feed dogs. Using a 1.5mm zigzag stitch and invisible thread on top, zigzag lightly around the circle.

14 Repeat all steps for the remaining circle quilts.

Quantities listed below are for all four circle quilt projects. Specific fabric and cut sizes appear with each project.

IF YOU PURCHASE THE BACKGROUND FABRIC

THREAD

 --- 40-weight polyester or rayon thread
 --- 60-weight gray and white bobbin fill
 --- Clear polyester invisible thread

NOTIONS

 --- 6" wooden or plastic machine embroidery hoop
 --- Black 1.0 and .005 Micron Pigma pen
 --- Exacto knife
 --- Fray check & small paint brush
 --- 80 Microtex sharp needles
 --- Water-soluble glue
 --- Muslin or scrap fabric

STABILIZER AND TULLE

 --- 10" x 60" water-soluble stabilizer film
 --- 10" x 110" water-soluble stabilizer backing
 --- 10" x 80" gray or silver tulle

NOTE: Extra stabilizers and tulle are recommended to make samples.

IF YOU ARE APPLIQUÉING YOUR OWN BACKGROUND

THREAD

 --- 40-weight polyester or rayon thread
 --- 60-weight gray and white bobbin fill
 --- Clear polyester invisible thread
 --- Backing & appliqué thread to match backing

NOTIONS

 --- 6" wooden or plastic machine embroidery hoop
 --- Black 1.0 and .005 Micron Pigma pen
 --- Freezer paper
 --- Exacto knife
 --- 3 sheets paper–backed fusible web
 --- Fray check & small paint brush
 --- 80 Microtex sharp needles
 --- Water-soluble glue
 --- Muslin or scrap fabric

STABILIZER AND TULLE

 --- 10" x 60" water-soluble stabilizer film
 --- 10" x 110" water-soluble stabilizer backing
 --- 10" x 80" gray or silver tulle

NOTE: Extra stabilizers and tulle are recommended to make samples.

ASSEMBLING THE BACKGROUND

Note: If you are assembling your own background fabric, omit the chimney as it is too small to accurately trace and fuse.

Fusible Appliqué

❶ Tape the master pattern from page 81 with the back of the pattern face up to a light box or sunny window. Position the fusible web on top, paper-side up. Trace the bodies of the house and 2 barns. Trace the roofs and silo separately. Trace the small shrubs at the barns and house. Trace the path. Fuse each piece to the wrong side of the specific fabric. Cut out.

❷ Lay the pieces back on the master pattern. Lightly trace the windows, doors, and lines of the house and roof onto the fabric with a mechanical pencil. Repeat for the roofs for the barns and silo.

❸ Use either the Pigma pen or a small pointed paint brush and the Cool Gray Tsukineko ink to lightly draw over the tracings of the house and barns lines, the windows, and doors and the lines on the silo.

❹ If using the Tsukineko inks, dip the shader brush into the Gray Tsukineko and rub off most of the ink on a piece of scrap fabric. Ink in the shading under the eaves of the barns and house and under the roof on the porch. Sporadically shade all 3 of the roofs. Use the Sand ink to repeat for the silo and door on the barn; use the Lemon ink with a fine point brush to paint the color in the windows on the house. Use the color photo for guidance.

SPRING'S MORNING

Finished size with circle border approximately 11" x 11"

Omit the Notions below and Assembling the Background if you purchase the background fabric online (see Resources on page 127).

NOTIONS

- – – – Cool Gray, Sand, and Lemon Tsukineko ink or corresponding colors in fabric paint
- – – – Fantastix pointed dauber or ¼" shader paint brush
- – – – Fine point paint brush
- – – – 12" x 12" piece of freezer paper
- – – – Scraps: small print sky fabric; green/yellow batik for foreground and mountains; red batik for barns; brown batik for silo; white for the house; brown batik for gardens; pale tan for path; and pale gray batik for roof

Appliqué

1 With the master pattern facing up, trace the template for the sky, hills, fields, 3 gardens, and the foreground onto the dull side of freezer paper. Press the templates to the right side of the specific fabric.

2 Trace around each template and cut out, leaving a generous $1/4$" seam allowance on all interior seams and $3/4$" around the outside circle perimeter.

3 Appliqué the sky, upper and middle hills, and the fields and the gardens to the right and left of the house. Fuse the small barn in place, then the roof on the barn and the small shrubs in front of the barn. Fuse the house in place and the two roofs on the house; a light box works well here to make sure the location is correct. The idea is to fuse the house in place along the ridge before the next appliqué piece is stitched in place.

4 Fuse the path to the foreground. Appliqué the remaining pieces together. Fuse the large barn, roof, silo, and shrubs into position above the large garden. Use a .005 Pigma pen to draw the small foreground posts and barbwire, making sure that no rails go across the end of the path. Draw the distant posts and barbwire to the left of the small barn.

Tracing and Hooping the Designs

1 Machine baste 1 piece of 2" x $8^1/2$" muslin to the right side of the fabric and 1 piece 2" x $10^1/2$" to the bottom. Press seams toward the muslin (measure for accuracy before cutting). Remove muslin when design is complete.

2 Lay the master pattern on a light box or sunny window and position the background fabric on top. Tape both in place. Line up Tree 1 to the left of the house and Trees 2 and 3 to the right of the large barn. Trace the 3 trunks and canopies with a mechanical pencil onto the background fabric.

3 Cut 2 pieces of 10" x 10" clear water-soluble stabilizer and trace the foreground flowers and fence with barbwire onto one of them. Trace the bottom of the fence posts, barbwire, and flowers about $1/4$" into the seam allowance. (Use the Sharpie or 1.0 Pigma pen.)

4 Take the second piece of stabilizer film and trace the bottom part of the flowers and stems that overlap the border circle.

5 See chapter 5, page 41, for Direct method hooping instructions.

Small Trees at the House and Barns

1 Hoop the design, encompassing all 3 trees. Make sure the stabilizer fits underneath the muslin strips.

Figure 1
Thread paint Trunks 1, 2, and 3 by following the drawing of the trunks.

Figure 2
Thread paint the 1st canopy color on Tree 1 with thread #2.

Figure 3
Thread paint the 1st canopy color on Tree 2 with Thread #3.

❷ Trees 1, 2, and 3—See Thread #1 and figure 1. With the trees facing you, move the hoop north to south to fill in the trunks and branches. Take care that the thread in Tree 1 doesn't stitch into the house or barn, as this tree is behind both.

❸ Tree 1—See Thread #2 and figure 2. With the Tree 1 canopy facing you, move the hoop erratically north to south and east to west to lightly thread paint the 1st canopy color (diagram 1). This is a small stitch because of the size of the tree.

❹ Trees 1 and 2—See Thread #3. Repeat Step 3 to thread paint the 1st canopy color on Tree 2 (figure 3). On Tree 1, repeat Step 3, this time thread painting between the stitches already in place (figure 4).

❺ Trees 1, 2, and 3—See Thread #4. Repeat Step 3 to thread paint the 3rd canopy color on Tree 1 (figure 5). Repeat Step 3 to thread paint the 2nd thread color on Tree 2 (figure 6). Repeat Step 2 to thread paint the 1st canopy color for Tree #3 (figure 6).

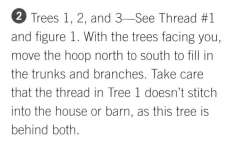

Diagram 1
Meander the straight stitch irregularly around the canopy.

Figure 4
Thread paint the 2nd thread color on Tree 1 with Thread 3.

Figure 5
Thread paint the 3rd canopy color on Tree 1 with Thread #4.

Figure 6
Thread paint the 2nd canopy color on Tree 2 and the 1st canopy color on Tree 3 with Thread #4.

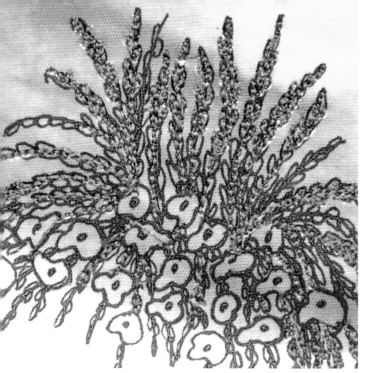

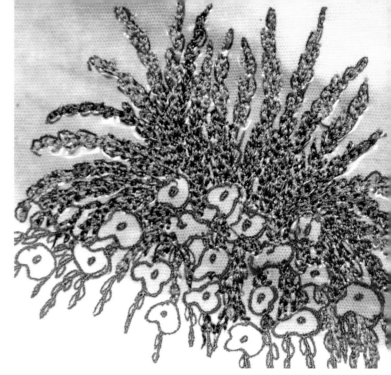

Figure 7
Make a backward loop to form the left leaf and a forward loop to form the right leaf for the medium-green thread.

Figure 8
Repeat the "loop" movement to form the dark-green loops.

Diagram 2
Close up of backward & forward loops, enlarged greatly.

Foreground Flower Stems

1 See Thread #5 and figure 7. Notice on the master pattern that I have drawn small leaves on each stem. Should you find this too difficult to master, simply thread paint out to the end of the stem and then back; you will get the same look. See what the completed stitch looks like in diagram 2. To execute the stitch, start at the spine of the stem and make a backwards loop for the left leaf and a forward loop for the right leaf. Thread paint up the stem repeating the motion to make all the stems and leaves. This is a very small stitch. If the loop is too large, the leaves will be too big for the area. Practice first to get the idea before thread painting onto the fabric.

2 To get from stem to stem so there are not so many jump stitches, stitch all the way down the stem to the base and stitch over to the next stem. Repeat, completing all stems as shown in figure 7. Vary the thread, making some the entire stem and others just part of the stem as there is a darker green to add.

3 See Thread #6 and figure 8. Repeat Steps 1 and 2 following the drawing on the master pattern. Again, make some of the dark-green stitches go all the way up the stem and have others meet the medium-green stitches. The idea here is to meander the color around the stems.

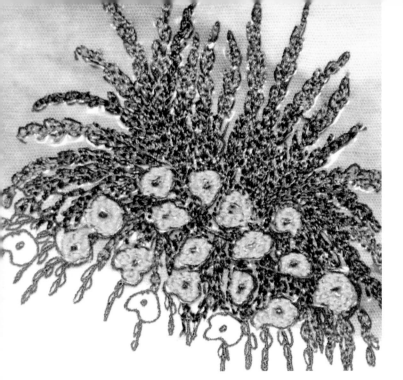

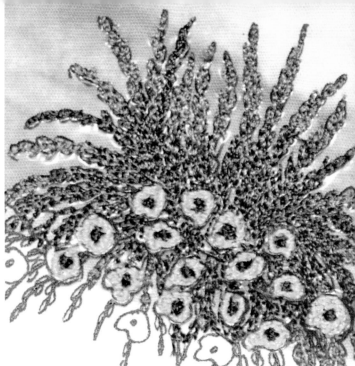

Figure 9
Move the hoop in a clockwise movement to form a small circular satin stitch.

Figure 10
Repeat for center of flower.

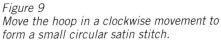

Diagram 3
#1 partial zigzag stitch; #2 flower petal complete; #3 flower center complete.

Yellow Foreground Flowers

1 See Thread #7 and figure 9. With the hoop facing you, locate the first flower. Moving the hoop very slowly in a clockwise fashion, satin stitch around the outside edge of the flower. See diagram 3 for steps on how the stitch looks. Continue moving the hoop around the circle until all holes are thread painted. Don't cover up the center. Raise the needle and position it on the outside edge of the next flower. Repeat until all flowers are complete.

2 See Thread #8 and figure 10. Move the hoop in a small circle to fill the center (Diagram 3).

Posts and Barbwire

1 See Thread #9 and figure 11 for Steps 1–3. With the fence facing you, move the hoop slowly, following the drawn line of the barbwire. At the barb, barely move the hoop north then south to form a small blob of thread. Keep the movement small. Beginning and ending stitches should start and end in the posts.

2 See Thread #10. With the first post facing you, underlay it. Repeat Steps 2–7 for the 2nd post while the thread is on the machine.

3 See Thread #11. With posts on their sides, thread paint the right side of the posts as shown in figure 11. Keep the left edge irregular to allow the next thread to blend into it. Thread paint all 3 colors about $1/4$" into the bottom seam allowance.

4 See Thread #12 and figure 12. Repeat Step 3, but this time thread paint Thread #12 into Thread #11 slightly to help blend the colors. Again keep the inside edge of Thread #12 irregular. Stop the thread where the post meets the cap.

5 See Thread #13 and figure 13. Repeat Step 4 to thread paint the 3rd color. Rotate the hoop a quarter of a turn and use the sketch stitch to fill in any holes.

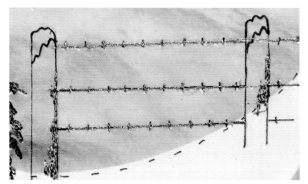

Figure 11
Move the hoop right to left very slowly to stitch the barbwire. Underlay (not shown) the posts. Thread paint the 1st post color.

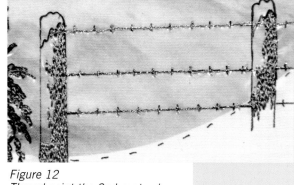

Figure 12
Thread paint the 2nd post color into the 1st post color 1.

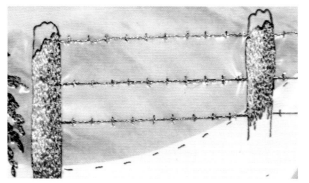

Figure 13
Thread paint post color 3 into color 2.

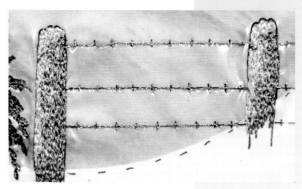

Figure 14
Post and caps complete. Line between post and cap.

6 See Thread #14 and figure 14 for Steps 6–7. With the design on its side, move the hoop right to left to fill in the caps on the posts.

7 See Thread #11 and figure 14. Using a straight stitch make an irregular stitch between the cap and the post to make it easier to see where the cap starts and the post stops.

8 Refer to chapter 5, page 38, to remove the stabilizer from the thread appliqués.

Adding the Circle Border

1 Refer to chapter 10, page 68 to add the circle border.

2 Before adding the outside borders, also in chapter 10, the yellow flowers and stems that overlap the border circle need to be thread painted:

a. Place 1 piece of 10" x 10" water-soluble stabilizer backing behind the fabric underneath the flowers.
b. Place the drawn-on stabilizer in position on top of the background fabric and hoop it.
c. Repeat Steps 1–3 under Foreground Flower Stems and Steps 1–2 under Yellow Foreground Flowers to thread paint the flowers and stems (pages 77-78).
d. Cut away the excess stabilizer and rinse to remove it. It is not necessary to soak the design as long as the border is well rinsed.

Thread Chart for SPRING'S MORNING

Thread number	Design	Thread color	Stitch selection	Stitch width	Hoop movement
1 Trees 1, 2, & 3	Trunk color	Medium yellow brown	Straight		Follow trunk, Figure 1
2 Tree 1	1st color canopy	Dark green	Straight		Zigzag meander, Figure 2
3 Trees 1 & 2	1st color canopy – Tree 2 2nd color canopy – Tree 1	Medium green	Straight		Same, Figure 3 Figure 4
4 Trees 1, 2, & 3	3rd color canopy – Tree 1 2nd color canopy – Tree 2 1st color canopy – Tree 3	Light green	Straight		Same, Figure 5 Figure 6 Figure 6
5 Flower stems	1st color stem	Medium green	Straight		Follow drawing, Figure 7 & Diagram 2
6	2nd color stem	Dark green	Straight		Follow drawing, Figure 8
7 Flowers	Flowers	Bright yellow	Zigzag	1.0mm	Circular satin stitch, Figure 9, Diagram 3
8	Petal center	Dark brown	Zigzag		Same, Figure 10
9 Barbwire	Barbwire	Metallic silver	Straight		Follow drawing, Figure 11
10 Fence	Underlay	Clear invisible	Straight		1/8" parallel lines Figure 11
11	1st color post	Dark gray	Zigzag	1.75mm	R–L Figure 11
12	2nd color post	Medium taupe	Zigzag		R–L Figure 12
13	3rd color post	Light tan	Zigzag		R–L Figure 13
14	Fence caps	Cream	Zigzag	1.0mm	Circular satin stitch, Figure 14

Master pattern for
SPRING'S MORNING—*100%*

A Summer Day

Finished size with circle border approximately 11" x 11"

Omit the Notions below and Assembling the Background if you purchase the background fabric online (see Resources on page 127).

NOTIONS

– – – Scraps of small-print sky fabric; beige batik for walkway; various green/beige batiks for the hills and foreground

ASSEMBLING THE BACKGROUND

Note: The printed house is available on my website.

❶ Trace the sky, hills, foreground (trace the foreground in one piece), and walkway from the master pattern on page 90 onto the dull side of freezer paper. Cut out the templates and press the freezer paper to the right side of the selected fabric. Trace around each template with a pencil and cut out, leaving a generous $1/4$" seam allowance on all interior seams and $3/4$" around the outside circle perimeter.

❷ Appliqué the walkway on top of the foreground fabric; appliqué the hills together, then the foreground to the hills and the sky to the hills. Press. Draw the distant fence onto the background fabric with a black or gray Pigma pen.

❸ Fuse a piece of fusible web slightly larger than the printed house to the back of the printed house fabric following manufacturer's directions. Lay the house on a cutting board. Using a sharp X-Acto® knife, carefully cut away the space between the house and the last porch post first. Carefully cut out the rest of the house with scissors. Fuse in position on the background fabric.

TRACING AND HOOPING THE DESIGNS

❶ Machine baste the (2) 2" x $8^{1/2}$" pieces of muslin to each side of the fabric and a 2" x $10^{1/2}$" piece to the top. Press seams toward the muslin. Remove muslin when the top is complete.

❷ Lay the master pattern on a light box or sunny window and position the background fabric on top. Tape both in place. With a mechanical pencil trace the tree to the right of the house on the background fabric and the evergreen to the left. Lightly trace the branches and canopy for the overhanging bough.

3 Cut 1 piece 10" x 10" of clear water-soluble stabilizer film and trace the fence and mailbox. Snug the right fence post underneath the larger one as shown in Figure 11. To allow shrinkage, trace the ends of the rails 1/2" past the background circle as shown on the master pattern. Trace the grass under the fence, snuggling the grass together.

4 Cut 2 pieces 10" x 10" of gray or silver tulle.

5 Cut 3 pieces 10" x 10" of water-soluble stabilizer backing.

6 See chapter 5, page 41, for Direct method hooping instructions and page 37 for the Tulle Sandwich method.

STITCHING THE DIRECT METHOD DESIGNS

Note: Pay attention to the thread numbers for Threads 1–7 in the Thread Chart on page 89. In several instances 2 or more parts of the design are thread painted before moving to the next thread color.

Trunks and Branches for Trees

1 See Thread #1 and figure 1 for the Evergreen Steps 1–3. Rotate the hoop so the tree is facing you. Insert the needle on the right bottom of the evergreen trunk. Pull the hoop toward you very slowly to form a decreasing satin stitch. About 1/3 of the way up the trunk, reduce the width to 1.5. Pull the hoop another third and reduce the width to about 1.0 mm. Continue pulling the hoop and reducing the width until the width reaches

Figure 1
Use a tapering satin stitch to thread paint the evergreen trunk. Thread paint the small deciduous trunk by following the drawn line.

around .5mm at the top of the tree. Travel back down the trunk if there are any holes, this time increasing the width.

2 Thread paint the deciduous tree branches by following the drawn line. Don't let the stitches for the trunk infringe on the house roof.

3 Thread paint an irregular line of stitches for the dirt at the side and front of the house by moving the hoop right to left slowly along the side of the house. The line should be about 2 to 3 threads thick and about 1/8" away from the side of the house. At the corner where the house meets the front of the porch, thread paint a straight line. At the steps, raise the needle and hop the thread over the steps, finishing the dirt to the right of the steps.

Figure 2
With the evergreen facing you, move the hoop irregularly north to south stitching from one side of the evergreen bough to the other.

Figure 3
Notice the irregular stitches on the evergreen and the first canopy color on the small tree. Scribble the small dirt and shrubs at the side and front of the house.

Evergreen Boughs

❶ See Thread #2 and figures 2 and 3. With the evergreen tree facing you, use the sketch stitch to make very erratic north to south stitches. Stitch from the outside bough on one side to the other all the way down the trunk leaving about ¼" of the trunk exposed at the bottom. The bottom right boughs will infringe on the side of the house (figure 3).

❷ Shrubs—Make some small scribble stitches along the side of the house (figure 3). The shrubs at the front of the

Figure 4
Notice the 2nd bough color on the evergreen and the canopy's 2nd color. Thread paint the flowers at the side and front of the house.

house should be a straight line. Hop the thread over the steps.

❸ Evergreen—See Thread #3 and figure 4. Repeat Step 1 to thread paint the 2nd bough color, lightly filling in between the stitches already in place.

❹ See Thread #4 and figure 5. With the tree facing you, move the hoop erratically to form the dirt under the tree.

Deciduous Tree to the Right of the House

❶ See Thread #5 and figure 3. With the canopy facing you move the hoop randomly right to left and up and down to thread paint the 1st canopy color (diagram 1). Meander around the canopy leaving some space for the next thread.

Figure 5
Evergreen, small tree, and house shrubs are complete. Add dirt under evergreen.

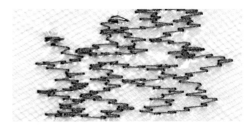

Diagram 1
Move the hoop erratically right to left, north to south to form the stitch.

Figure 6
Follow the drawn line to thread paint the branches using a straight stitch.

2 See Thread #6 and figure 4. Repeat Step 1, thread painting in between the stitches already in place.

3 See Thread #7 and figure 4. Scribble stitch small flowers on top of the shrubs reducing the size at the front of the house.

Large Branches and Canopy

Note: The sun in this project is to the left. In figures 7–9, notice that space was reserved on the left side of the canopy for the lighter thread colors.

1 See Thread #8 and figure 6. Thread paint the branches by following the drawn line. Thread paint ½" into the seam allowance.

2 See Thread #9 and figure 7. With the canopy facing you, move the hoop irregularly right to left and up and down to form the 1st canopy color (diagram 1). This is an erratic meandering stitch, so don't make the stitching lines too close together. Refer to figures 7–10 for each color location.

3 See Thread #10 and figure 8 for Steps 4–5. Repeat Step 2, thread painting between the stitches already in place.

Figure 7
Move the hoop right to left to thread paint canopy color #1. Leave the canopy's left side for the lighter thread colors.

Figure 8
Move the hoop right to left to thread paint canopy #2 and #3, filling between the spaces already in place.

Figure 9
Repeat for Thread #4.

Figure 10
Canopy complete.

❹ See Thread #11. Repeat Step 2 to thread paint between the stitches already in place. Notice the beginnings of the lighter thread to the left side of the canopy.

❺ See Thread #12 and figure 9. Reduce the width to 1.0mm. This time instead of meandering around the canopy, hop-scotch the color around the canopy.

❻ See Thread #13 and figure 10. Repeat Step 5, making sure that the outside left edges of the canopy are concentrated, especially if using a very light color thread.

STITCHING THE TULLE SANDWICH DESIGNS

Fence and Mailbox

Posts and Rails

❶ See Thread #14 and figure 11. With the fence post and mailbox post facing you, underlay them. Rotate the hoop so the posts are on their sides and underlay the rails and the mailbox.

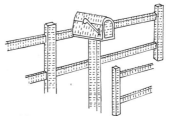

Figure 11
Underlay the posts, rails, and mailbox. Notice the direction of the stitches.

❷ See Thread #15 and figure 12. With the mailbox facing you, thread paint the bottom line of the mailbox by moving the hoop right to left. At the mailbox door, rotate the hoop slightly to thread paint the area under the door. At the arch around the door, rotate the hoop to keep the line parallel to you to thread paint the arch. Switch to a straight stitch if the zigzag is too difficult to control around the arch. Outline the posts, caps of posts, rails, and where the posts meet the ground (figure 13). Outline the mailbox except for the bolt and flag.

Figure 12
Outline the fence and fill the bottom line of the mailbox and the arc around the door.

Figure 13
Thread paint the 1st post and rail color.

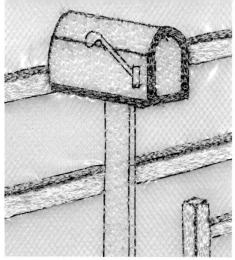

Figure 14
Fill the top of the rails. Thread paint the 2nd post and rail color.

Figure 15
Thread paint the 3rd post and rail color and the front of the mailbox post.

❸ See Thread #16 and figure 13. With the rails facing you, move the hoop right to left to fill about ¹/₃ of the surface of the rails and all of the post caps. Rotate the hoop so the posts are on their side and fill in about ¹/₃ of the posts. Make sure the outside edges are solid.

❹ See Thread # 17 and figure 14 for Steps 4–5. Rotate the hoop so the rails are facing you and move the hoop right to left, carefully filling the narrow gray top of the rails.

❺ See Thread #18. Repeat Step 3, thread painting in between the stitches already in place for the 2nd rail and post color.

❻ See Thread #19 and figure 15. Repeat Step 3, filling in the rest of the rails and posts.

❼ Use Thread #16 to fill in any remaining holes using the sketch stitch.

Mailbox
❶ See Thread #20 and figure 15. Rotate the hoop so the mailbox post is on its side and move the hoop right to left to shade the narrow front of the post. With the post facing you fill in the holes using the sketch stitch.

❷ See Thread #21 and figure 16 for Steps 2–3. Repeat Step 1 filling in the surface of the side post.

❸ See Thread #22. With the side of the mailbox facing you move the hoop right to left to fill in the side and top of the mailbox, maneuvering the stitches around the flag and bolt. Rotate the hoop so the bottom of the mailbox door is parallel to you. Thread paint the door just bumping the right and left stitches into the dark gray arch around the door.

Flag
❶ See Thread #23 and figure 17. With the edge of the flag parallel to you, move the hoop right to left to fill in the stem of the flag. At the arch at the top of the flag make a small satin stitch following the arch of the flag.

Bolt
❶ See Thread #24. Make a test of the bolt in the free space outside the design to test for the appropriate zigzag width and length. Start at the top of the bolt and pull the hoop toward you very slowly to make a small satin stitch.

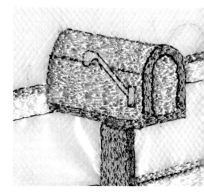

Figure 16
Move the hoop right to left to fill the mailbox and door. Rotate the hoop one-quarter turn to thread paint the side of the post.

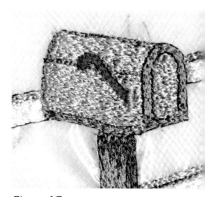

Figure 17
Follow the line of the flag to thread paint the flag. Use a small satin stitch to stitch the bolt.

Figure 18
Shade and highlight the mailbox and post. Mailbox and fence complete.

Shading and Highlighting

1 See Thread #25 and figure 18 for Steps 1–5. With the mailbox facing you, move the hoop right to left to shade the body of the mailbox where it meets the arc on the top front. Randomly shade the door and the mailbox side.

2 See Thread #26. On the top and side of the mailbox highlight the left top and side of the mailbox, making stitches heavy enough to see.

3 See Thread #27. Randomly highlight the side of the post using the sketch stitch.

4 See Thread #28. With the post facing you, stitch some dark shading where the post meets the mailbox.

5 Use Threads #15–22 and the sketch stitch to fill in the remaining holes in the fence and mailbox.

Figure 19
Thread paint the 1st grass color. Vertical lines should be irregular. Keep the base dense.

Figure 20
Stitch the 2nd & 3rd grass color irregularly and between the grass already in place.

Grass at the Fence

1 See Thread #29 and figure 19. Rotate the hoop so the grass is on its side and thread paint the grass in an irregular fashion. Make some lines tall and some short, keeping the grass dense at the base.

2 See Thread #30 and figure 20 for Steps 2–3. Thread paint the 2nd grass color between the grass already in place, again making some tall and some short.

3 See Thread #31. Repeat Step 2 to complete the grass.

4 Refer to chapter 5, page 38, to remove the stabilizer and tulle from the thread appliqués.

Inserting the Fences and Grasses into the Seam Allowance

1 Lay the master pattern on a light box and place the background fabric in position on top.

2 Lay the fences and grasses in position on top of the background fabric.

3 Put a dot of water-soluble glue on the back of the fences and grasses just at the area where their edges go into the seam allowance. Let dry.

4 Permanently attach the fence to the quilt top after quilting is complete.

Adding the Circle Border

1 Refer to chapter 10, page 68, to add the circle border and the outside borders. The edges of the fences, post, and grasses should be caught in the seam allowance.

2 Let the top of the grass remain three-dimensional.

Thread Chart for A Summer Day

Thread number	Design	Thread color	Stitch selection	Stitch width	Hoop movement
1 Small tree trunks	Evergreen trunk	Medium brown	Zigzag	1.75–.05mm	Tapering satin stitch
Tree branches	Deciduous tree branches		Straight		Follow branches
Dirt	Dirt at side of house		Straight		Scribble
2 Evergreen boughs	1st color boughs	Dark green	Straight		Sketch stitch
Shrubs at house	1st color shrubs at house		Straight		Scribble
3 Evergreen	2nd color canopy	Medium spruce	Straight		Sketch stitch
4 Dirt	Dirt under evergreen	Medium yellow brown	Zigzag	1.0mm	Random zigzag
5 Decidous canopy	1st color canopy	Dark green	Zigzag		Meander R–L
6	2nd color canopy	Bright olive	Zigzag		Same
7 House flowers	Gold house flowers	Dark gold	Straight		Scribble
8 Large canopy	Branches	Medium brown	Straight		Follow line of branches
9	1st color canopy	Dark olive	Zigzag	2.5mm	Random zigzag
10	2nd color canopy	Medium light olive	Zigzag		Same
11	3rd color canopy	Light olive	Zigzag		Same
12	4th color canopy	Medium gold	Zigzag	1.0mm	Same
13	5th color canopy	Pale olive	Zigzag		Same
14 Fence & mailbox	Underlay fence & mailbox	Clear invisible	Straight		1/8" parallel lines
15	Bottom edge & arch of mailbox	Dark gray	Zigzag	1.0mm	R–L keep line parallel at arch on mailbox door
	Outline fence & mailbox		Straight		Follow outline
16	1st color fence	White	Zigzag	2.0mm	R–L
17	Fill top of rail	Light gray	Zigzag	1.0mm	R–L
18	2nd color fence	Cream	Zigzag	2.0mm	R–L
19	3rd color fence	Light gray	Zigzag		R–L
20 Mailbox	Shade front of post	Dark taupe	Zigzag	1.25mm	R–L
21	Side of post	Medium brown	Zigzag	2.0mm	R–L
22	Body of mailbox	Medium gray	Zigzag	1.5mm	R–L
23	Flag	Medium red	Zigzag	.5mm	R–L
24	Mailbox bolt	Bright orange	Zigzag	1.0mm	Satin stitch
25	Shade mailbox	Medium dark gray	Straight		Sketch stitch
26	Highlight mailbox	White	Straight		Same
27	Highlight post	Cream	Straight		Same
28	Shade post	Dark brown	Straight		Same
29 Grass at fence	1st color grass	Dark green	Zigzag	1.5mm	Follow drawn line
30	2nd color grass	Light olive	Zigzag		Same
31	3rd color grass	Medium olive	Zigzag		Same

Master pattern for
A SUMMER DAY—*100%*

Grass at Fence

Thread Painting with Style NANCY PRINCE

Fusible Appliqué

1 With the back of the pattern facing up, tape the master pattern on page 99 to a light box or sunny window. Position the fusible paper-backed web on top, paper-side up. Trace the 2 barns, the house, and the silo. Trace the roofs for the barns and house and the round cap on the silo separately. Fuse each piece to the wrong side of the specific fabric. Cut out.

2 Lay the pieces back on the master pattern. With a mechanical pencil trace the door, windows, and lines of the house, barns, roofs, and silo.

3 Practicing first, use either the .005 gray or black Pigma pen or a small pointed paint brush and the Cool Gray Tsukineko ink to lightly draw over the tracings of the house and barn lines, windows, doors, and the lines on the silo.

4 To shade the buildings, lightly paint under the eaves of the barns and house with Cool Gray Tsukineko ink. Sporadically shade all 3 of the roofs; use the Sand ink to repeat for the silo and door on the barn (use a fine point brush for this exercise). Use the color photo for suggestions.

Appliqué

1 With the master pattern facing up, trace the sky, mountains, foreground (cut the foreground in one piece), roadway, and garden onto the dull side of freezer paper. Cut out the templates and press the freezer paper to the right side of the selected fabric. Trace around the tem-

GOLDEN DAYS

Finished size with circle border approximately 11" x 11"

Omit the Notions below and Assembling the Background if you purchase the background fabric online (see Resources on page 127).

NOTIONS

– – – Scraps: small print sky fabric; multicolored beige batik for the roadway and silo; multicolored medium to light-green batik for the foreground and mountains; multicolored red and gray batik for the barns; white for the house; and brown/gold batik for the garden

– – – Cool Gray and Sand Tsukineko inks or fabric paint to augment the fabric

plates and cut out, leaving a generous $1/4$" seam allowance on all interior seams and $3/4$" around the outside circle perimeter. Cut out.

② Appliqué the roadway and garden in place on top of the foreground fabric. Appliqué the mountains together and the mountains to the sky.

③ Fuse the house, barns, and silo in place in front of the mountains. Fuse the roofs on the barns and the round dome on the silo. Appliqué the foreground to the mountains. Clip all interior curves and press.

TRACING AND HOOPING THE DESIGNS

① Machine baste the 2 muslin 2" x $8^{1/2}$" pieces to each side of the fabric and the 2" x $11^{1/2}$" piece to the top. Press seams toward the muslin. Remove the muslin when the top is complete.

② Lay the master pattern on a light box or sunny window and position the background fabric on top. Tape in place.

Make sure the barns are lined up so that the small tree left of the barn will be in the right place. Trace the canopy and trunk onto the background fabric with a mechanical pencil.

③ Cut 1 piece of 10" x 12" clear water-soluble stabilizer film. Trace the large tree trunk, the fence, and the pumpkins onto the center of the stabilizer. To minimize the number of hoopings, group the designs about $1/2$" apart. To allow for shrinkage, trace the top part of the trunk $1/2$" past the outside of the perimeter circle as shown on the master pattern.

④ Cut 1 piece of 3" x 3" clear stabilizer. Lay it over the words on the sign and trace the letters.

⑤ Cut 2 pieces of 10" x 12" stabilizer backing.

⑥ See chapter 5, page 41, for Direct method hooping instructions and page 37 for Tulle Sandwich instructions. Make sure the stabilizer backing is underneath the muslin pieces.

STITCHING THE DIRECT METHOD DESIGNS

Small Tree Left of the Barn

① Hoop the small tree left of the barn. See Thread #1 and figure 1. With the design facing you, move the hoop north to south filling in about 50 percent of the trunk. Complete all the small branches with Thread #1.

② See Thread #2 and figure 2 for Steps 2–3. Repeat Step 2, filling in between the stitches already in place.

③ See Thread #3. Rotate the hoop so the canopy is facing you. While moving

Figure 1
Trace the canopy onto the background fabric. Thread paint the 1st trunk color.

Figure 2
Fill the 2nd color on the tree trunk and the 1st canopy color.

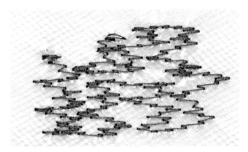

Diagram 1
Move the hoop right to left and up and down erratically to form the stitch.

the hoop right to left, pull it toward you at the same time so that the stitches meander around the canopy (diagram 1). The amount of stitches depends on how thick you want the foliage to be. This is a fall tree so don't make the first color too heavy.

4 See Thread #4 and figure 3 for Steps 4–5. Repeat Step 3, thread painting in between the stitches already in place.

5 See Thread # 5. Repeat Step 4 to complete the canopy.

Garden and Roadway

1 See Thread #6. Hoop the garden. Lightly scribble stitch some grass along the bottom and right edge of the garden. Keep in mind that the height of the grass will be shorter the further away the area is from you. See the master pattern for scribble suggestions.

2 See Thread #7. Lightly sketch over the first stitches around the garden making sure the thread is not too dense.

3 See Thread #6. Reposition the hoop on the right side of the roadway. Repeat Step 1 for both sides of the roadway. The grass on the right side of the quilt should be the tallest, gradually getting smaller until the stitches on the far left of the quilt are a continuous straight line.

Figure 3
Small canopy complete.

4 Reposition the hoop and repeat Steps 1–3 to complete the roadway grass.

STITCHING THE TULLE SANDWICH METHOD DESIGNS

Large Tree Trunk

1 Hoop the design so the bottom of the trunk is in the hoop. Note: complete all 4 thread colors before moving the hoop to complete the top portion of the trunk.

2 See Thread #8 and figure 4. Rotate the hoop so the trunk is facing you. Underlay the trunk.

Figure 4
Underlay the trunk.

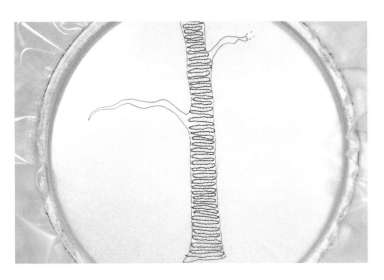

Figure 5
Rotate the hoop so the tree is on its side and thread paint the 1st trunk color.

Figure 6
Thread paint the 2nd trunk color blending into the 1st trunk color.

Figure 7
Trunk complete.

❸ See figure 5. Switch to a zigzag stitch and rotate the hoop so the trunk is lying on its side. Move the hoop randomly right to left making the left side of the trunk solid. Fill about one third of the trunk. Make the right outside stitches irregular so it is easier for Thread #9 to blend into Thread #8. At the right and left branches reduce the width to 2mm and partially fill in the branches. Arc the hoop to keep the line you are thread painting parallel to you. As the limbs get smaller reduce the width to 1mm. Switch to a straight stitch if it is too difficult to use a small zigzag to thread paint the small branches.

❹ See Thread #9 and figure 6. For the 2nd trunk color intertwine some of Thread #9 into Thread #8 so there is an irregular line between the two threads. Try and stitch this step so one line diffuses into another. The sketch stitch will be used once all 4 colors are thread painted in place to soften the edges between one color and another.

❺ See Thread #10. Repeat Steps 3–4.

❻ See Thread #11 and figure 7. Repeat Steps 3–4.

❼ Evaluate the design. Rotate the hoop so the design is facing you and use the sketch stitch to fill in any remaining holes and soften the edges between colors. Use all 4 colors if necessary to tweak the trunk (figure 7).

❽ Reposition the hoop and repeat Steps 1–7 for the upper trunk.

Pumpkins

Note: While each thread is on the machine, complete all 10 pumpkins using the specific thread color. Pumpkin figures only show the detail on the 3 largest pumpkins.

❶ Rotate the hoop so the pumpkins are facing you.

❷ See Thread #12 and figure 8 for Steps 2–4. Outline all the pumpkins by following the curve of each pumpkin, moving the hoop slowly to build up the thread.

❸ See Thread #13. Underlay the 3 large pumpkins.

❹ Thread paint a straight line from the stem down the center of all the pumpkins. This indicates where the thread lines should be straight up and down.

❺ Rotate the pumpkin so it is on its right side. Stitch to the right side of the pumpkin. Arc the hoop to follow the curve of the pumpkin. Continue arcing the hoop right to left until you get close to the straight line in the center. Then manipulate the hoop so you blend the curved stitches into the straight ones, as in the center pumpkin in figure 9. Thread paint to the left side and repeat.

❻ With the design facing you, use the sketch stitch to fill in any holes.

❼ Repeat for the 9 remaining pumpkins until all pumpkins are filled.

❽ See Thread #14 and figure 10 for Steps 8–9. Highlight the top of each pumpkin by following the arc of the pumpkin.

❾ See Thread #15. Follow the outline of each stem to fill in.

Figure 8
Outline the pumpkins; underlay the front 3 pumpkins, thread paint a straight line down the center. Right side of the pumpkin partially done. Notice the arc of the thread on the right pumpkin.

Figure 9
Thread paint the right side of the pumpkin arcing the thread. Stitch to left and repeat. Blend the curve of the pumpkin into the straight center line.

Figure 10
With the pumpkin facing you thread paint the highlight and the stem at the top of each pumpkin.

Fence

1 See Thread #16 and figure 11. Underlay the posts and rails. Notice in figure 11 that the underlay on the posts is stitched east to west and the rails north to south.

2 See figure 12. Rotate the hoop so the posts are on their side and thread paint about ¹/₃ of the surface of both posts by moving the hoop right to left. The tops of each post are thread painted later with Thread #18.

3 Rotate the hoop so the rails are facing you and thread paint about ¹/₃ of the surface of all the rails.

4 See Thread #17 and figure 13. Repeat Steps 2–3 to thread paint the 2nd thread color, stitching in between the stitches already in place.

5 See Thread #18 and figure 14 for Steps 5–8. Repeat Steps 2–4 for the 3rd thread color.

6 Reduce the width to .5mm. Rotate the hoop so the posts are facing you. Make a small circular satin stitch to fill in the cap on each post. To execute the stitch move the hoop slowly in a clockwise motion. Once the perimeter of the cap is thread painted, move the hoop right to left to fill in the center.

7 See Thread #19. Thread paint in the ditch where the rails go into the posts to slightly shade this area.

8 Use the sketch stitch to fill any holes.

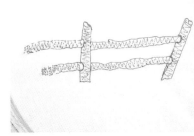

Figure 11
Underlay the fence. Note the stitches on the posts are going east to west and on the rails, north to south.

Figure 12
Fill ¹/₃ of the posts and rails with the 1st fence color. Note the direction of the thread.

Figure 13
Thread paint the 2nd fence color.

Figure 14
Fill the final spaces on the rails and posts with the 3rd fence color.

Figure 15
With the sign facing you move the hoop right to left to fill about 50% of the board. Rotate a quarter of a turn to fill 50% of the post.

Figure 16
Thread paint optional weathering color and the 2nd sign color.

Figure 17
Highlight the left side of the board and post.

Figure 18
Lay the stabilizer with the traced words on top of the completed sign. Pin in place.

Figure 19
Thread paint the letters. Sign complete.

"Punkins for Sale" Sign

❶ See Thread #20 and figure 15. With the sign on its side underlay the board, then rotate one-quarter turn and underlay the post. With the sign facing you, move the hoop right to left to fill in about 50 percent of the board, then rotate one-quarter turn and fill about 50 percent of the post.

❷ Optional Step. See Thread #21 and figure 16. With the sign on its side, irregularly move the hoop right to left to fill in a small portion of the post. The idea here is to give some weathering to the post; rotate one-quarter turn and repeat for the board.

❸ See Thread #22 and figure 16. With the sign facing you, fill in between the threads already in place on the board; rotate one-quarter turn and repeat for the post.

❹ See Thread #23 and figure 17 for Steps 4–5. Lightly and irregularly shade the post where it meets the sign. Stitch in the ditch at the top of the post for more shading.

❺ See Thread #24 and figure 17. Add highlights, making the stitches irregular on the left side of the sign. Thread paint the thread heavily enough so it can be seen.

❻ See figure 18. Lay the drawn-on stabilizer with the words over the thread-painted sign. Pin in place around the sign to secure.

❼ See Thread #25 and figure 19. Very carefully thread paint the P. When done, raise the presser foot to the up position. With your left forefinger pull out about 1"

of thread from the spool so the jump stitch isn't so short. Lower the foot while putting some pressure on the thread around your finger. Drop the presser foot, keeping the pressure on the thread and thread paint the 2nd letter.

❽ Repeat Step 7 until all the letters are done.

❾ Refer to chapter 5, page 38, to remove the stabilizer and tulle from the thread appliqués.

ATTACHING THE LARGE TRUNK TO THE QUILT TOP

❶ Put a few drops of water-soluble glue on the back of the trunk from the bottom branches up but don't glue down the bottom of the trunk yet. The bottom part of the trunk is glued and stitched down after the quilt is quilted.

❷ Refer to chapter 5, page 40, to attach the top of the trunk to the quilt top.

LARGE CANOPY

❶ Lay the master pattern on a light box or sunny window and tape to secure it. Lay the background fabric over the pattern; tape and lightly pencil draw the outline of the canopy and the smaller branches on the quilt top. Due to shrinkage of the trunk, the limbs may no longer match exactly the limbs on the master pattern. Improvise a bit here to line up the small branches to the larger ones.

❷ Hoop the design so the top left of the canopy is in the hoop.

③ See Thread #8 and figure 20. Thread paint the small branches on the tree by using a 1mm stitch width and following the pencil drawing. Switch to a straight stitch if necessary to thread paint the smaller branches.

④ See Thread #26 and figure 21 for Steps 4–5. Moving the hoop right to left, randomly thread paint some background green, (see diagram 1 for the specific execution of the stitch). Don't concentrate the thread too much in one area.

⑤ See Thread #27. Randomly thread paint the 2nd canopy color as shown in figure 21, thread painting in between the stitches already in place.

⑥ See Thread #28. Repeat Step 5 to thread paint the 3rd canopy color.

⑦ See Thread #29 and figure 22. Repeat Step 5 to thread paint the 4th canopy color.

⑧ Reposition the hoop if necessary to complete any part of the canopy that might not have fit into the hoop.

⑨ Repeat Steps 3–8 to complete the canopy.

⑩ Remove the stabilizer (see chapter 5, page 38).

INSERTING THE FENCE INTO THE SEAM ALLOWANCE

① Lay the master pattern on a light box and place the background fabric in position on top.

② Lay the fence in position on top of the background fabric.

③ Put a dot of water-soluble glue on the back of the fence just at the area where the edge of the fence goes into the seam allowance. Let dry.

ADDING THE CIRCLE BORDER

① Refer to chapter 10, page 68, to add the circle border and the outside borders. The left edge of the fence should be caught in the seam allowance.

② Refer to chapter 5, page 40, to attach the thread appliqués.

From left to right:

Figure 20
Thread paint the small branches on the tree.

Figure 21
Move the hoop right to left to irregularly thread paint the first two canopy colors.

Figure 22
Canopy complete.

Thread Chart for GOLDEN DAYS

Thread number	Design	Thread color	Stitch selection	Stitch width	Hoop movement
1 Tree left of barn	1st color trunk	Medium tan	Straight		R–L follow trunk
2	2nd color trunk	Medium brown	Straight		Same
3 Small canopy	1st color canopy	Medium light olive	Zigzag	.75mm	R–L meander around canopy
4	2nd color canopy	Medium gold	Zigzag		Same
5	3rd color canopy	Light gold	Zigzag		Same
6 Garden & roadway	1st color grass at garden Roadway grass	Medium light olive	Scribble		Scribble Same
7	2nd color grass at garden	Medium olive	Scribble		Same
8 Large tree trunk	Underlay 1st color trunk	Dark brown	Straight Zigzag	3.0–1.0mm	1/8" parallel lines R–L
9	2nd color trunk	Medium brown	Zigzag		Same
10	3rd color trunk	Medium taupe	Zigzag		Same
11	4th color trunk	Light taupe	Zigzag		Same
12 Pumpkins	Outline	Dark orange	Straight		Follow outline
13	Underlay Fill	Medium orange	Straight		1/8" parallel lines Follow outline
14	Highlight top of pumpkins	Bight yellow	Straight		Same
15	Pumpkin stem	Medium brown	Straight		Follow outline
16 Fence	Underlay 1st color fence	Medium gray	Straight Zigzag	2.0mm	1/8" parallel lines R–L to fill
17	2nd color fence	Medium tan	Zigzag		Same
18	3rd color fence	Light tan	Zigzag		Same
19	Shade where rails meet posts	Dark brown	Straight		In the ditch where rail meets posts
20 Punkins Sign	Underlay 1st color board & post	Medium light taupe	Straight Zigzag	2.0mm	1/8" parallel lines R–L
21 Optional	2nd color board & post	Medium brown	Zigzag		Same
22	3rd color board & post	Medium light gray	Zigzag		Same
23	Shade post	Charcoal	Straight		Same
24	Highlight	Créme	Straight		Same
25	Letters	Black	Straight		Follow letters
26 Large canopy	1st color canopy	Medium olive	Zigzag	2.5mm	Meander around canopy
27	2nd color canopy	Medium light red	Zigzag		Same
28	3rd color canopy	Medium orange	Zigzag		Same
29	4th color canopy	Bright yellow	Zigzag		Same

Master pattern for
GOLDEN DAYS—*100%*

FIRST SNOWFALL

Finished size with circle border approximately 11" x 11"

Omit the Notions below and Assembling the Background if you purchase the background fabric online (see Resources on page 127).

NOTIONS

– – – Cool Gray and Sky Blue Tsukineko ink or gray or sky blue fabric paint
– – – Fantastik pointed dauber or $1/2$" shader paint brush
– – – Scraps: small print sky fabric; solid white fabric; and multicolored red fabric
– – – Fine point paint brush

ASSEMBLING THE BACKGROUND

Note: If you are assembling your own background fabric, omit the chimney and smoke as they are too small to accurately trace and fuse.

Fusible Appliqué

Tape the master pattern on page 107 with the back of the pattern face up to a light box or sunny window. Position the fusible web on top, paper-side up; trace the house and roof separately. Fuse the body of the house to the wrong side of the red batik and the roof to the white fabric. Cut out.

Appliqué

1 With the master pattern face up, trace the template for the sky and snowy foreground onto the dull side of a piece of freezer paper. Cut out.

2 Press the templates to the right side of the specific fabric—sky to small print sky; foreground to white "snowy" fabric. Trace around the templates. Remove the templates.

3 Cut out the sky and foreground fabric leaving a generous $1/4$" seam allowance on all interior seams and $3/4$" on the perimeter seams.

4 Appliqué the foreground to the sky. Press.

5 Place the appliquéd background on a light box and lightly pencil the terrain lines on the white foreground. Trace the 3 trees at the house onto the background fabric. Fuse the body of the house to the background fabric.

6 Use the .005 Pigma pen to draw in the windows and the eave lines. Use the Cool Gray ink or gray fabric paint and a fine paint brush to shade the house under the eaves and sporadically on the roof.

7 See the master pattern and completed quilt for suggestions on how the terrain lines should look. Lightly ink or paint the terrain lines. It is best to ink the lines first as lightly as possible and build the ink up.

8 Using the Cool Gray ink or fabric paint and a fine point paint brush lightly paint the 3 small trees by the house.

9 Take the Sky Blue Tsukineko ink or fabric paint, put about ¹/₈ teaspoon into a small cup and add a small amount of water. Rub off most of the ink and follow the painted or drawn lines to paint a little blue shading along the contour lines using the shader brush.

10 Continue playing with the two colors of ink or paint until satisfied. Heat set with an iron once the paint is dry.

TRACING AND HOOPING THE DESIGNS

1 Machine baste 1 piece of 2" x 8¹/₂" muslin to the right side of the fabric and 1 piece 2" x 11¹/₂" to the top. Press seams toward the muslin (measure for accuracy before cutting). Remove muslin when design is complete.

2 Cut 1 piece of 10" x 12" clear water-soluble stabilizer film and trace the birch trees, evergreens, fence, snowman, and shovel onto the stabilizer. To minimize the number of hoopings, group the designs about ¹/₂" to 1" apart. Trace all the designs. Trace the top part of the birch trunks and the right side of the fence post ½" past the outside of the circle to allow for shrinkage.

3 Cut 1 piece 10" x 12" of stabilizer backing.

4 Cut 2 pieces 10" x12" of gray tulle.

5 See chapter 5, page 37, for Tulle Sandwich hooping instructions.

STITCHING THE TULLE SANDWICH DESIGNS

Birch Trees

1 See Thread #1 and figure 1. Insert a white bobbin and a size 80 needle. Hoop the birch trees. Rotate the hoop so the birch trees are lying on their sides. Underlay the trunks running the stitches from the base to the tops of the trunk. Do not underlay the 3 small branches.

2 See Thread #2 and figure 2 for Steps 2–4. Rotate the hoop so one of the boughs is facing you and move the hoop slowly right to left to fill in the snow on the limbs. Repeat for the other limbs.

3 See Thread #3. With the trees on their side, locate a dark bark line at the bottom of the left tree. Move the hoop slowly right to left along the length of the line to form the dark bark. Raise the needle and move to the next dark bark area.

4 Repeat Step 3 until all the dark areas of the bark are done on both trees. Cut connecting threads.

5 See Thread #4 and figure 3. With the tree facing you, move the hoop right to left bumping the outside drawn lines of the trunk. As you go up the tree, keep the lines of stitches about ¹/₈" apart, remembering that there are 2 more thread colors to go so don't fill too heavy. This is not a satin stitch but a gradual right to left motion up the trunk.

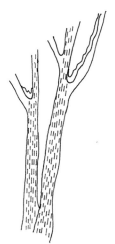

Figure 1
Underlay the trunks. Notice the stitches run from the base to the top of the tree.

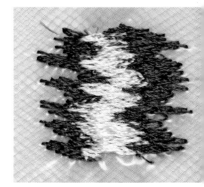

Diagram 1
Stitch for evergreen boughs and snow.

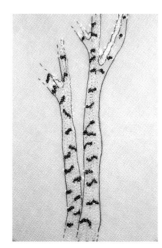

Figure 2
Fill in the snow on the branches and the dark lines on the trunk and branches.

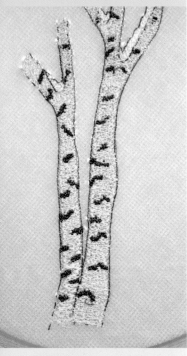

Figure 3
With the tree facing you move the hoop right to left to partially fill in the 1st trunk color.

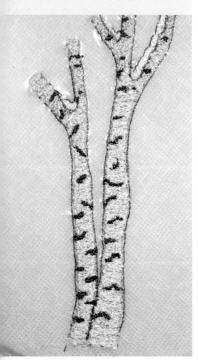

Figure 4
Birch trunk complete.

6 At the first left branch reduce the width to 1.0mm and rotate the hoop counterclockwise so the threads move gradually from a right to left northern orientation to a more leftward orientation. Continue to rotate the hoop so the area you are thread painting is facing you.

7 Maneuver around the dark bark lines as carefully as possible. Should some be infringed upon, they can be touched up at the end. Repeat for the 2nd trunk.

8 See Thread #5. Repeat Steps 5–7 to thread paint the 2nd trunk color. Fill in between the stitches already in place but leaving some space for Thread #6.

9 See Thread #6 and figure 4. Repeat Steps 5–7 filling in between the stitches already in place especially along the edges. Once all 3 colors are thread painted rotate the hoop so the trunk is on its side and using the sketch stitch fill in all remaining holes.

10 Use Thread #3 and a straight stitch to touch up the dark bark if necessary.

11 Reposition the hoop if necessary and repeat Steps 1–10 to complete any unfinished part of the tree.

Evergreen Trees

1 See Thread #1 and figure 5 for Steps 1–2. Underlay the 4 evergreens. Note: Figures show only one evergreen.

2 See Thread #7 and figure 5. Rotate the hoop so the trees are on their side. Move the hoop right to left in an irregular fashion so the top and bottom dark green of the boughs have jagged edges (see the dark green example on the left in diagram 1). This is a very small stitch. Once one

set of boughs are done, stitch to the next one. The snow will cover up the stitches from one bough to another.

3 Repeat for the other 3 evergreens.

4 See Thread #8 and figures 6 and 7. Start at the top of the tree and slowly move the hoop right to left filling in the top. At the first green bough thread paint the snow slightly into the branches. Keep moving the hoop right to left filling in the snow until you reach the underside of the first branch. Thread paint the snow slightly into the green branches above (see the green example on the right in diagram 1). Repeat to complete the tree. Repeat for the other 3 evergreens.

Figure 5
Rotate the hoop so the trees are on their side and thread paint the green boughs.

Figure 6
Partial snow on evergreen.

Figure 7
Evergreen complete.

Figure 8
Evergreen tree with shading.

5 Option: Figure 8 gives an idea of how to shade the tree and is an option since these trees are so small.

Fence

1 See Thread #1 and figure 9. Insert a gray bobbin. With the fence facing you, move the hoop right to left to underlay the post; then rotate the hoop so the post is on its side and underlay the rails.

2 See Thread #9 and figure 10. Rotate the hoop so the post is on its side; move the hoop right to left to thread paint the post covering about 1/3 of the surface area. Rotate the hoop so the fence is facing you and repeat to fill in 1/3 of the rails.

3 See Thread #10. Repeat Step 2, thread painting in between the stitches already in place.

4 See Thread #11 and figure 11. Repeat Steps 2–3.

5 See Thread #12 and figure 11 for Steps 5–6. With the fence facing you, move the hoop right to left filling in the snow on top of the rails. Make sure outside edges are solid.

6 See Thread #13. Stitch in the ditch where the rails meet the post to form a shadow there.

Snowman and Shovel

1 See Thread #14. Rotate the hoop so the snowman is facing you and underlay the snowman; underlay the shovel blade with the blade facing you.

2 See Thread #15 and figure 12 for Steps 2–5. Locate the bottom button on the body. To fill it, move the hoop in small circles following the outline of the drawn button. Raise the needle and locate the second button. Repeat until all buttons on the body are done.

3 Switch to a straight stitch and follow the lines for the eyes, mouth, and under the brim of the hat to fill. Outline the mouth 2 times.

4 See Thread #16. Follow the outline of the nose to fill.

5 See Thread #17. Thread paint the pipe stem 2 or 3 times. At the pipe bowl, switch to a 1.25mm zigzag. Pull the hoop toward you very slowly making a satin stitch to form the bowl. This is a very small movement, so practice first.

6 See Thread #18. Switch to a white bobbin. Using a straight stitch make a vertical line up the lower and middle body and the head. This shows the center of the body where the stitches should be straight up and down.

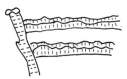

Figure 9
Underlay the post and rails with Thread #1. Notice the stitches run right to left across the post and north to south on the rails.

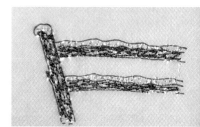

Figure 10
Thread paint the 1st rail and post color. Notice the direction of the stitches on the post and rails.

Figure 11
Thread paint the snow on the rails. Rails complete. Stitch in the ditch between the post and rails.

Figure 12
With a zigzag stitch fill the buttons. Fill the eyes, mouth and under the brim of hat with a straight stitch.

Figure 13
Rotate the hoop so the
snowman is on its side and
partially fill in the body and
head of the snowman.

Figure 14
Fill in the hat, arms, buttons,
and shovel. Shade the body,
under the hat and the top of
the vest.

Figure 15
Fill the shovel handle, lines on
the shovel blade, vest, and hat
brim and outline the scarf.

Figure 16
Snowman and shovel
complete.

7 See figure 13 for Steps 7–8. Switch to a 1.5mm zigzag. Rotate the hoop so the snowman is on its right side. Rotate the hoop clockwise then counterclockwise following the curve of the body. You will be making a backwards "C." Continue this backward movement until about $\frac{1}{8}$" from the straight line in the center. At the center straight line blend the arc of the curve into the straight line at the center. Bump to the line separating the lower body from the middle body. Navigate around the buttons so as not to cover them up. The buttons can be touched up at completion if infringed upon.

8 Stitch to the left side of the body and repeat Step 7; this time the rotation of the hoop is a "C" movement. Cover about 75 percent of the surface of the bottom body. Stitch up to the center body and repeat the stitch movement reducing the width to 1.0mm. Repeat for the head, carefully navigating around the eyes, nose, mouth, and pipe.

9 See Thread #19 and figure 14 for Steps 9–17. Rotate the hoop so the snowman is on its right side. Follow the drawings on the master pattern and shade the lower body at the waist and the right side of the bottom, underneath the scarf, and underneath the hat brim using the sketch stitch. To shade the lower body, move the hoop right to left bumping to the waistline above and having the bottom edge of the stitch irregular. Remember it is easier to add more shading at completion than to take threads out.

10 Rotate the shovel so it is on its side and fill in the entire shovel blade, moving the hoop right to left.

11 Evaluate the body and continue using Threads #18 and #19 to fill and shade the body and head.

12 Touch up the buttons, mouth, etc., with Thread #15.

13 See Thread #20. Switch to a gray bobbin. Outline the hat twice. Rotate the hoop so the shovel is on its side. Following the lines on the master pattern, make 3 to 4 lines in the shovel (figure 15). Cut connecting threads.

14 See Thread #21. Rotate the hoop so the snowman is facing you and move the hoop right to left to fill in the brim. Rotate one-quarter turn and fill in the top of the hat, moving the hoop slowly right to left.

15 See Thread #22. Following the outlines of the right arm fill in the arm. Repeat for the left arm.

16 See Thread #23. Rotate the hoop so the snowman is facing you and move the hoop in small circles to fill in the buttons on the right side of the vest.

17 See Thread #24. Rotate the hoop so the snowman is on its side and follow the vest's shading lines on the master pattern to shade. Bump the threads to the shoulders and make the bottom threads irregular.

18 See Thread #25 and figure 15 for Steps 18–22. With the snowman on its side, move the hoop right to left filling in the vest. At the shading area stitch some of the blending red into the shading red. Rotate the hoop so the snowman is facing you and fill in any holes in the vest with the sketch stitch.

19 With the shovel on its side, move the hoop right to left to fill in the handle.

At the circular top, move the hoop very slowly in a circle making a small satin stitch around the handle to fill it. Adjust the zigzag width so that the right and left swings of the needle hit the outside and inside drawn line.

20 To fill the hatband, rotate the hoop so the snowman is facing you and move the hoop right to left.

21 Evaluate the vest, shovel handle, and hat band; use Thread #25 and the sketch stitch to fill any holes. Use Thread #24 and the sketch stitch to stitch the final vest shade.

22 See Thread#26. Outline the scarf twice.

23 See Thread #27 and figure 16 for Steps 23–25. Rotate the hoop so the snowman is facing you; move the hoop right to left to fill in the scarf, bumping into the dark-green outline.

24 See Thread #28. Follow the outline of the flower petals on the hat with the needle to satin stitch around the edges.

25 See Thread #29. Move the hoop in small circles to fill the center of the flower.

26 Refer to chapter 5, page 38, to remove the stabilizer and tulle from the thread appliqués.

INSERTING THE FENCE AND THE TOP OF THE BIRCH TREES

1 Lay the master pattern on a light box and place the background fabric on top.

2 Lay the fence and birch trees on top of the background fabric.

3 Put a dot of water-soluble glue on the back of the fence and tree tops just at the area where the edge of the fence and the trees go into the seam allowance. Make sure that the fence and the birch trees line up with the cuts in the fabric (Step 1 below). Let dry.

4 Do not stitch the fence or trees in place; do this after the quilting is complete.

PREPARING THE QUILT FOR THE THREAD APPLIQUÉS

1 Mark the right and left points for the shovel on the quilt top lightly with a pencil. See the master pattern for locations. Repeat for the bottom of the snowman, the fence post, the birch trees, and the two attached evergreens. Lay the quilt top on a cutting mat. Using a sharp X-Acto knife, make a slit into the background fabric slightly larger than the two pencil marks at the shovel location. Make sure the knife is sharp to avoid fraying the fabric. Repeat for the snowman, fence post, and birch trees. This allows the designs to slide underneath the slit after quilting so they look more realistic. Note: Before cutting into the fabric, lay your thread appliqués into position to make sure they fit into the specified area.

2 Take an old paint brush and carefully apply Fray Check™ sealant to the cut edges. Let dry.

ADDING THE CIRCLE BORDER

1 Refer to chapter 10, page 68, to add the circle borders and the outside borders.

2 Refer to Chapter 5, page 40, to attach the thread appliqués.

Thread Chart for First Snowfall

Thread number	Design	Thread color	Stitch selection	Stitch width	Hoop movement
1 Birch tree	Underlay	Clear invisible	Straight		1/8" parallel lines: tree on its side
2	Snow on limbs	White	Zigzag	.5mm	R–L follow limb
3	Dark bark	Dark gray	Zigzag	.75mm	R–L along the line
4	1st color trunk	Medium tan	Zigzag	1.5–1.0mm	R–L
5	2nd color trunk	Light gray	Zigzag		Same
6	3rd color trunk	White	Zigzag		Same
7 Evergreens	Boughs	Dark green	Zigzag	.5mm	R–L along boughs
8	Snow on boughs	White	Zigzag		Same
9 Fence	1st color fence	Dark taupe	Zigzag	1.5mm	R–L
10	2nd color fence	Medium brown	Zigzag		Same
11	3rd color fence	Light gray	Zigzag		Same
12	Snow on rails	White	Zigzag		Same
13	Shade rails at posts	Charcoal	Straight		Follow curve of rails
14 Snowman & shovel	Underlay	Clear invisible	Straight		1/8" parallel lines
15	Buttons Eyes, mouth, under brim	Charcoal	Zigzag Straight	.25mm	Rotate in circles Follow drawn line
16	Nose	Medium orange	Straight		Follow outline
17	Pipe stem Pipe bowl	Medium gold	Straight Zigzag	 1.25mm	Follow outline Vertical satin stitch
18	Body centerline Fill body	White	Straight Zigzag	 1.5mm	N–S for center line R–L for zigzag
19	Body shading Shovel blade	Light gray	Zigzag Zigzag	1.25mm 2.0mm	See master pattern R–L
20 Hat	Outline hats Lines on shovel blade	Dark gray	Straight Straight		Follow outline Follow pattern
21	Fill hat brim and hat	Medium gray	Zigzag	1.5mm	R–L
22 Arms	Fill arms	Dark brown	Zigzag	1.0mm	Follow drawing
23 Buttons on vest	Buttons on vest	Bright gold	Zigzag	.25mm	Make small circles
24 Vest	Shade vest	Cranberry	Zigzag	.5mm	See master pattern
25	Fill vest Shovel handle Hat band	Medium red	Zigzag Zigzag Zigzag	1.25mm	R–L Follow handle R–L
26 Scarf	Outline scarf	Dark green	Straight		Follow outline
27	Fill scarf	Medium green	Zigzag	1.0mm	R–L
28 Flower	Flower petals	Dark gold	Zigzag	.75mm	Follow outline
29	Flower center	Medium green	Zigzag	.25mm	Rotate in circles

Note: The pencil lines on the snowman are shading lines.

Dotted lines below birch trees indicate that this area is under the fabric. The 2 dots along the terrian line are the right and left locations of the large and small evergreens and the 2 dots below are the centers of the remaining evergreens.

Master pattern for
FIRST SNOWFALL—100%

SEARCHING FOR BUTTERFFLIES

Finished size
approximately 16" x 20½"

Omit Notions 1–4 and Fabric for the flowers, stems, leaves, and buds on page 109 and Fusing the Flower Appliqué on page 110 if you purchased the background fabric on-line (see Resources on page 127).

THREAD

- – – 40-weight polyester or rayon thread
- – – 60-weight gray bobbin thread
- – – Clear polyester invisible thread
- – – Thread to match the backing

NOTIONS

- - - Cool Gray Tsukineko ink or medium-gray fabric paint
- - - Pointed Fantastix brush or 1/4" shader paint brush
- - - X-Acto knife
- - - 2–3 sheets of paper-backed fusible web
- - - Water-soluble glue
- - - Mechanical pencil and marking pencil
- - - Black ultra fine point Sharpie or 1.0 Micron Pigma pen
- - - 5" length of thin gauge wire
- - - Size 80 Microtex needle
- - - 2 pieces of 10" x 10" gray or silver tulle
- - - 1 piece of 10" x 10" water-soluble stabilizer backing
- - - 1 piece of 10" x 10" water-soluble stabilizer film
- - - 6" wooden or plastic machine embroidery hoop

FABRIC

- - - Background, outer borders, and binding – 3/4 yard green batik
- - - Backing fabric – 1/2 yard
- - - Batting – 3/4 yard
- - - Inner border – fat quarter of pink batik
- - - Flower – fat quarter of multicolored pink batik
- - - Flower center – scrap of blue/pink batik
- - - Flower stem and bud – fat quarter of brown/green batik
- - - Leaves and buds – scraps of different complementary green and brown batiks
- - - Flower buds – fat quarter of yellow/green batik

CUTTING ORDER

Green Batik
2 strips 2¼" x 42" for binding
1 piece 12" x 16" long for background
2 pieces 2½" x 17" for outer side borders
2 pieces 2½" x 25" for outer top and bottom borders

Pink Batik
2 pieces 1" x 14" for inner side borders
2 pieces 1" x 19" for inner top and
   bottom borders

Batting
24" x 29"

Backing
23" x 18"

FUSING THE FLOWER APPLIQUÉ

Note: Instructions assume fusible appliqué.

1 Tape the master pattern on page 116 with the back of the pattern facing up to a light box or sunny window. Position the fusible paper-backed web on top, paper-side up. Trace the flower petals, flower center, stems, and flower buds onto the paper side of the fusible web. Trace the flower center as one piece. Trace each leaf separately. Add ⅛" to any edge that fits underneath another leaf. Cut out.

2 Press each template to the wrong side of the specific fabric. Cut out each piece.

3 Remove the paper backing from the fusible web.

4 Lay the master pattern over a light box with the pattern facing up and trace the lines inside the flower center. These interior lines will be used as a guide to quilt the flower center. Remove the flower center.

5 Place the green batik background on top. Position each appliqué piece in place. Slide a hard surface underneath the fabric (so the pieces won't be disturbed while moving to the ironing board). Remove the board and fuse the pieces in place.

6 If desired, zigzag each piece in place with a 1mm zigzag stitch.

7 Use the Cool Gray Tsukineko ink or gray fabric paint to shade the flower petal leaves where needed. See chapter 9, pages 61-62, and chapter 10 for more specifics on using Tsukineko inks. Shade the leaves and buds to your liking.

TRACING AND HOOPING THE BUTTERFLY DESIGNS

1 Cut 1 piece 10" x 10" clear water-soluble stabilizer film.

2 Cut 1 piece 10" x 10" water soluble stabilizer backing.

3 Cut 2 pieces 10" x 10" gray or silver tulle.

4 Lay the clear stabilizer film on top of the butterfly pattern and trace the design in the center of the stabilizer.

5 See chapter 5, page 37, for Tulle Sandwich hooping instructions.

Note: Threads #1–8 are thread painted using the straight stitch, so it doesn't matter where the hoop is in relation to you. No hoop direction is given for these steps except where a specific direction is advantageous. Before starting, see the blending examples in chapter 6.

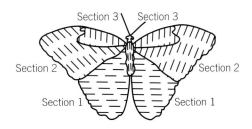

Figure 1
Thread 1— Underlay the butterfly. Notice the different directions of the underlay. The fill stitch will be perpendicular to the underlay.

BUTTERFLY

1 Underlay the butterfly—See Thread #1 and figure 1. Notice the direction of the underlay stitches in figure 1: Section 1–straight across; Section 2–at a slight angle; Section 3–perpendicular to Section 1. Remember when filling these areas with the threads below to rotate the hoop so the fill stitch is perpendicular to the underlay stitches.

2 First blue—See Thread #2 and figure 2. Thread paint all the interior lines of the blue section of the wing by following the drawn lines on each wing. Move the hoop very slowly to allow enough time for the thread to slightly build up on each line. Where the bottom of the blue wing meets the dark part of the bottom wing, move the hoop north to south (sketch stitch) to irregularly thread paint the bottom of the blue wing (figure 3 and diagram 3, page 113).

3 Separating red line—See Thread #3 and figure 3. Thread paint the red line separating the top and bottom wing.

4 Second blue—See Thread #4 and figures 4 and 5. Notice how the 2nd blue bumps against the dark blue outline already stitched in place. Notice how the inside edges are irregular to allow the 3rd blue thread to blend into the 2nd blue thread.

Figure 2
Move the hoop slowly to outline the blue interior lines of the butterfly. At the lower part of the blue wing move the hoop irregularly up and down to form the bottom blue wing.

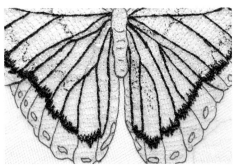

Figure 3
Notice the close-up of the 1st blue thread and the red line separating the top wing from the bottom wing.

Figure 4
Notice the location for the 2nd blue thread. Leave the inside edge of the thread irregular.

Figure 5
Close-up of the 2nd blue thread. Notice the change in thread directions from Sections 1 to 2. Also, notice how the 2nd blue bumps into the blue interior lines.

Figure 6
Full photo of the 3rd blue thread. Again blend one thread into another.

Figure 7
Close-up of the 3rd blue thread. Blend the 3rd blue thread into the 2nd blue thread.

Figure 8
4 blue threads complete.

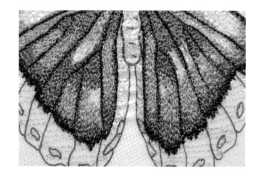

Figure 9
Outline the bottom and inner edge of the outside wing pulling the hoop very slowly to let the thread build up along the line.

5 Before changing each thread color, rotate the hoop so each individual section is facing you and use a sketch stitch to smooth the blending from thread to thread. Final tweaking will be done when the design is complete.

6 To get from wing space to wing space, stitch over the dark blue line. This line can be touched up at the end.

7 Third blue—See Thread #5 and figures 6 and 7. Repeat Steps 4–6, noting how the 3rd blue thread blends into the 2nd blue thread.

8 Fourth blue—See Thread #6 and figures 8 and 9. Repeat Steps 4–6 to thread paint the final blue thread.

9 Top of wing and center inside wing— See Thread #7 and figures 9 and 10. With the hoop facing you, move the hoop right to left following the outline of the top wing to fill it. Rotate the hoop so the body of the butterfly is on its side and fill the wings below the body.

10 Outline outside wing—See Thread #8 and figure 9. To outline the outside wing, slowly follow the drawn line to allow the thread to build up.

11 First outside wing—See Thread #9, figure 10, and diagrams 1 and 2. Start the stitching as shown in diagram 1. Thread paint down the left side of the outside line, moving the hoop right to left. Make a small satin stitch across the bottom of the wing, then up the right side, all the time slowly moving the hoop right to left to execute the stitch. Once the outline has been stitched, move the hoop right to left in an irregular fashion to thread paint about 1/3 of the bottom part of the wing (diagram 2). Navigate around the circles or ovals for the red and white dots on the wings. Stitch across the charcoal lines to get to the next section of the wing.

12 Second outside wing—See Thread #10 and figure 11. With the design on its side, move the hoop east to west blending into the dark blue thread above. Make the bottom lines of Thread #10 irregular. See diagram 4 for more detail.

13 Third outside wing—See Thread #11 and figure 12. Thread paint Thread #11 into Thread #10 above and into Thread #9 below blending into both thread colors. Navigate around the red and white dots.

14 Red dots on the wing—See Thread #12 and figure 13. With the wings facing you, move the hoop in a tight circle or oval to fill in the red dots. If you already thread painted over the dot area, simply thread paint the dots right over the threads already in place.

15 White dots on the wing —See Thread #13 and page 109. Repeat Step 14 to thread paint the white dots on the wing.

Figure 10
Thread paint the 1st outside wing color.
See diagrams 1 & 2 for execution of stitch.

Diagram 1

Figure 11
Thread paint the 2nd outside wing thread color blending this thread into the dark blue wing above.

Diagram 2

Figure 12
Blend the 3rd brown into the 1st brown below and the 2nd brown above.

Diagram 3

Figure 13
Move the hoop in a circle or oval to thread paint the red dots on the wing.

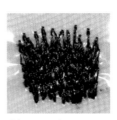

Diagram 4

Figure 14
Underlay the body again to stabilize the area where the satin stitch body goes.

Figure 15
Make a solid satin stitch to thread paint the body.

Figure 16
Start the satin stitch about ¹/₈" into the body to make the head. For the antennae, couch over a piece of wire.

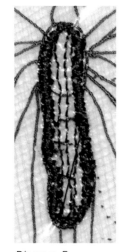

Diagram 5

Diagram 6

16 See Thread #14, figure 14, and diagram 5 to underlay the body. Set the zigzag width to 1.0mm and make a solid row of satin stitches around the entire body (not the head). This will give you some wiggle room in case you don't exactly hit the right zigzag width below (diagram 5).

17 With the butterfly facing you, start the zigzag stitch at 4.0mm. Note: Make a sample first to make sure the zigzag widths fit your design and to make sure you are pulling the hoop slowly enough. Concentrate on making a solid line of satin stitches for the body by pulling the hoop slowly towards you. Watch the right and left swing of the needle and as the size of the body increases, increase the width (diagram 6 and figure 15).

18 Lines on the body, top of the head and antennae—See Thread #15 and figure 16. See the master pattern for the location of the lines on the body. With the body facing you, move the hoop slowly right to left and carefully make the first lines on the butterfly body. Raise the needle and repeat for the other body lines.

19 Set the zigzag width to 3.0mm. With the head and antennae facing you, begin the head about ¹/₈" into the already stitched body (figure 16). Pull the hoop slowly towards you to make the stitch. Watch the right and left swing of the needle; as the area narrows, reduce the width. To make the right and left flares on the head, reduce the width to 1mm and slowly push the hoop away from you to form the stitch. Stitch back over the flare and thread paint to the center. Push the hoop away from you to make the left flare.

20 Cut 2 pieces of thin gauge wire 2" long for the antennae. Bump the left antenna in place at the head (figure 16) and take a few straight stitches to secure the wire in place. Switch to a 1.0mm zigzag and very slowly pull the hoop toward you to couch over the wire. Tack the stitch at the end with a straight stitch. Repeat for the right antenna. It is better to make the antennae too long than too short as this can be shortened at clean up.

21 See chapter 5, pages 38-39, to remove the stabilizer and tulle from the butterfly. Cut the antennae wire to size. Use the stencil cutter to fuse the end where the wire was cut. Bend the wire to shape.

Thread Chart for SEARCHING FOR BUTTERFLIES

Thread number	Design	Thread color	Stitch selection	Stitch width	Hoop movement
1 Wings	Underlay	Clear invisible	Straight		⅛" parallel lines Figure 1
2 Inside blue wing	1st color blue wing Outline interior wing and sketch bottom wing	Dark royal blue	Straight		Follow outline & Figure 2
3	Line between top and bottom wing	Medium red	Straight		Figure 3
4	2nd color blue wing	Medium-bright royal blue	Straight		Figures 4 & 5
5	3rd color blue wing	Medium-light royal blue	Straight		Figures 6 & 7
6	4th color blue wing	Pale royal blue	Straight		Figure 8
7	Top of wing and center body	Yellow brown	Straight		Figures 9 & 10
8 Outside brown wing	Outline outside wing	Charcoal	Straight		Figure 9
9	1st color outside wing	Dark taupe	Zigzag	1.0mm	Figure 10 & Diagrams 1 & 2
10	2nd color outside wing	Yellow brown	Zigzag		Figure 11
11	3rd color outside wing	Dark, dark brown	Zigzag		Figure 12
12	Dots on wings	Medium red	Zigzag		Oval or circle Figure 13
13		White	Zigzag		Oval or circle Figure 17
14	Underlay body (again)	Yellow brown	Straight		⅛" parallel lines Figure 14
	Fill body		Zigzag	4.0mm – 4.5mm – 3.5mm	Satin stitch body, Figure 15
15	Lines on body	Dark, dark brown	Straight		See master pattern
	Top of head		Zigzag	3.0mm – 2.0mm – 1.0mm	
	Antennae		Zigzag	1.0mm	Satin stitch

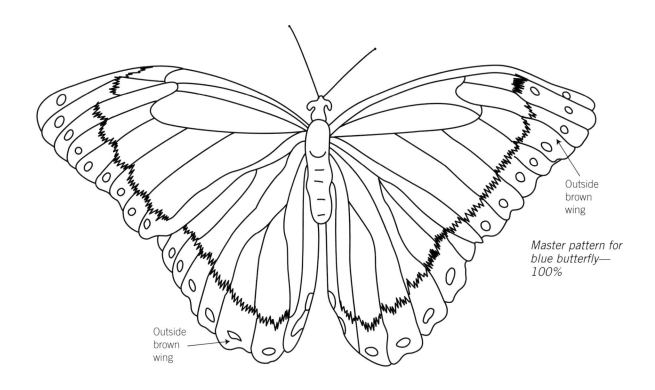

Outside
brown
wing

*Master pattern for
blue butterfly—
100%*

Outside
brown
wing

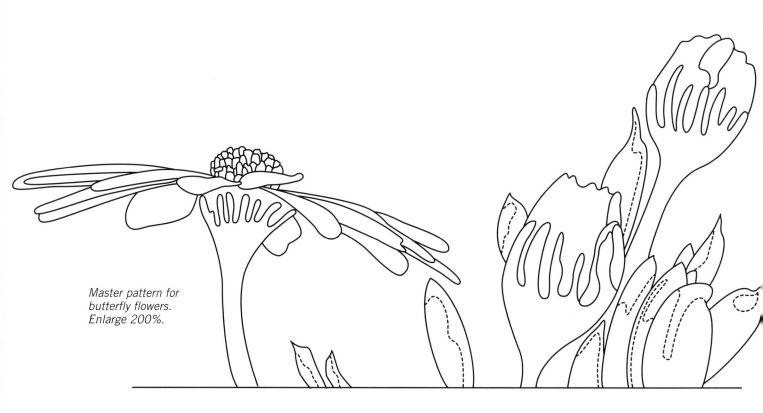

*Master pattern for
butterfly flowers.
Enlarge 200%.*

POPPIES ON PARADE

Finished size with border approximately 14" x 17"

The Direct method (pages 41) and a straight stitch (page 28) are used for this project.

THREAD

- – – 40-weight polyester or rayon thread
- – – 60-weight gray and white bobbin thread
- – – Clear polyester invisible thread
- – – Thread to match the backing

FABRIC, STABILIZER, AND NOTIONS

- – – Background – $3/4$ yard of cream Kona cotton
- – – Inner border – fat quarter of teal batik
- – – Outer border – fat quarter of light olive batik
- – – Backing – fat quarter
- – – 1 piece 15" x 13" lightweight fusible woven interfacing (only with Kona type fabric)
- – – 1 piece 15" x 13" water-soluble stabilizer backing
- – – 1 piece 16" x 13" clear water-soluble stabilizer film
- – – Prismacolor® Premiere® pencils – 3 or 4 shades of complementary greens, medium brown, yellow, sky blue, and pink
- – – 6" wooden or plastic machine embroidery hoop
- – – Black ultra fine point Sharpie or 1.0 Micron Pigma pen
- – – Size 80 Microtex needle
- – – Delta Ceramcoat® or Jo Sonja's® Textile Medium
- – – Versatex Fixer
- – – $1/2$" fabric paint brush

CUTTING ORDER

Cream
2 strips 2" x 17" for outer side borders
2 strips 2" x 20" for outer top and bottom borders
2 strips $2^{1}/4$" x 42" for binding
1 piece 17" x 13" for background

Teal
2 strips 1" x 13" (1st inner side borders)
2 strips 1" x 16" (1st inner top and bottom)

Light olive
2 strips 1" x 15" (outer side borders)
2 strips 1" x 18" (outer top and bottom)

Batting
22" x 26"

Backing
22" x 26"

CUTTING AND TRACING THE DESIGNS ONTO STABILIZER

1 Cut 1 piece of 15" x 13" lightweight fusible woven interfacing.

2 Cut 1 piece of 15" x 13" water-soluble stabilizer backing.

3 Cut 1 piece of 16" x 13" water stabilizer film.

4 Tape the master pattern to a flat surface and tape the stabilizer film on top. Trace the design with the Pigma pen or ultra fine point Sharpie.

Note: If the stabilizer backing is 10" wide, cut 2 pieces 10" x 16" and overlap them.

GETTING READY

1 Press the fusible interfacing to the back of the cream background fabric following manufacturer's directions.

2 Lay the stabilizer backing on a flat surface, then layer the Kona cotton with the drawn design on top.

3 Pin the layers in place.

4 Hoop the left poppies. Pin the excess fabric and stabilizers out of the way.

GENERAL INSTRUCTIONS

1 Randomly select the poppy flowers, stems, and leaf thread colors from Threads #1–7. The idea is to mix up the colors throughout. Use your discretion here.

2 To begin each stitch, bring the bobbin thread to the top, hold the thread tails, and begin stitching, making 5 or 6 stitches very close together to tack the beginning stitch. When ending the stitch, repeat, making 5 or 6 small stitches.

3 A number of the petals have small, very short vertical design lines on the back of the petals. Turn off the needle-down function. To execute the stitch, thread sketch over the 1st short line on the leftmost petal. Stitch back over the same line. To avoid very short connecting threads, hopscotch to another line at least ¼" away. Repeat to make the 2nd line and continue to hopscotch from line to line, cutting any connecting threads if they are in the way.

4 See the drawn lines on the master pattern for examples for the yellow and blue cloud formations; notice the dashed lines on the foreground and in the river. These lines are just an example where to use the colored pencils to augment the background fabric. Play with your creativity here when using the colored pencils.

5 Move the hoop slowly right to left when sketching the foreground and distant shrubs, the mountains, the dirt line at the river, the foreground shrubs at the river, and the line under the river shrubs to allow the thread to build up slightly.

6 Cut connecting threads when necessary so you don't stitch over them.

THREAD SKETCHING THE DESIGN

1 Petals—See Thread #1 and figure 1. Insert a gray bobbin. To execute the stitch, follow the outline of the first petal for the medium-red thread color. It will be necessary to stitch back over a line already sketched to get to the next petal. Continue randomly outlining petals until the selected medium–red flowers are complete.

2 See Thread #2 and figure 2 for Steps 2–3. Outline the charcoal flower center and then move the hoop right to left to fill

Figure 1
Outline of examples of all #1 red flower petals

Figure 2
Outline examples of all cranberry flower petals

Figure 3
Examples of coral petals (thread #3) complete. Green stems and leaves partially complete.

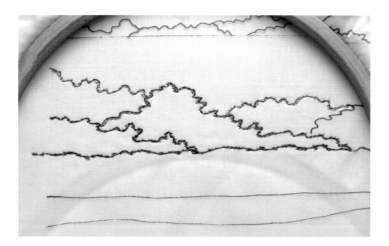

Figure 4
Left foreground shrubs complete.

the center. To sketch the anthers, start in the flower center and stitch out the anther; then stitch back over the same line to the center. Repeat for all flower centers.

3 See Thread #3. Repeat Step 1 to randomly sketch the cranberry color.

4 See Thread # 4 and figure 3 for Steps 4-10. Repeat Step 1 to finish outlining the poppy petals.

5 Stems and Leaves—See Thread #5. Locate the 1st leaf and stem color on the master pattern. Start at the base of the stem and sketch up the stem to the 1st grouping of leaves. Sketch out each leaf and back track over stitches where necessary to get back to the stem.

6 Continue sketching up the stem repeating Step 5 until the first flower stem is complete. Randomly select other stems and leaves for thread #5.

7 See Thread #6. Repeat Steps 5–6 to randomly sketch all Thread #6 leaves.

8 See Thread #7. Repeat Steps 5–6 to randomly sketch all Thread #7 leaves.

9 Rehoop and complete the remaining left and right poppies, at your discretion.

10 Reposition the hoop to encompass the left foreground shrubs at the river and the mountains. See figure 4 for Steps 10 and 11. The path will not be thread painted until time to do the river grass.

11 Left foreground shrubs—See Thread #8. To make the dirt, rotate the hoop so the shrubs are facing you. Move the hoop right to left to form the dirt areas under the shrubs. A slight build-up of thread here is good.

12 See Thread #9 and Shrubs 1 and 5 on the master pattern. To execute the stitch, follow the outline of Shrub #1 moving the hoop right to left to allow the thread to build up. Repeat for Shrub #5, noting that part of Shrub #5 is not in the hoop. Finish this shrub when hooping for the river grass in Step 31.

⓭ See Thread #10. Repeat Step 12 for Shrubs 2 and 4.

⓮ See Thread #11. Repeat Step 12 to complete Shrub 3.

⓯ See Thread #12. With the hoop facing you, move the hoop right to left to sketch the line under the river shrubs.

⓰ See Thread #13. Move the hoop right to left to outline Shrubs 6 and 8.

⓱ See Thread #14. Repeat Step 16 to outline Shrubs 7 and 9.

⓲ Distant mountains—See Thread #16 (a thread number was skipped for later use). Outline all the mountains in the hoop, moving the hoop right to left.

⓳ See Threads #17 and 18. The squiggles on the mountains can be sketched with either thread color. Choose the color at your discretion and follow the drawn line to sketch.

⓴ Reposition the hoop to encompass the center mountains and the river grass below (Figure 5).

㉑ See Thread #16. Outline the distant mountains. Sketch the river line separating the right and left sections of the distant shrubs.

㉒ See Threads #17-18 and repeat Step 19 to sketch the squiggles on the mountains.

㉓ Hills above the river—See Thread #19 and figure 5 for Steps 23-30. Outline the center hill and the beginning of the right hill.

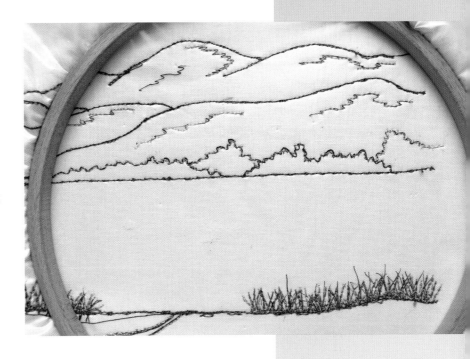

㉔ See Threads #20–21. Sketch the drawn line to make the squiggles on the mountain. Use either of the green colors at your discretion.

㉕ See Thread #12 and Step 15. Sketch the line under the river shrubs.

㉖ See Thread #14 and Step 15. Sketch the line under the river shrubs. See Thread #13 to sketch shrub 13 and Thread #15 to sketch shrub 12.

㉗ Dirt at river's edge—See Thread #8. Repeat Step 11 to sketch the dirt at the river's edge.

㉘ See Thread #22. With the grass facing you, sketch the 1st river grass color starting the stitch at the dirt, then stitching to the end of the grass and back to the dirt. At the base, make a few short up and down sketch stitches to get to the next grass line. Leave some spaces for the other 2 colors by stitching over 2–3 grass lines so the same grass colors are not next to each other. Repeat for all Thread #22 stitches.

Figure 5
Outline the mountains, hills, and distant shrubs at river. Sketch the grass at the river's edge.

㉙ See Thread #23–24. Repeat Step 28, sketching in between the threads already in place.

㉚ Finish foreground Shrub #5, following Step 12 on the foreground shrubs.

㉛ See Thread #25. Reposition the hoop to encompass as much of the path as possible. Start the sketch stitch at the river's edge on one side of the path. The beginning stitches at the river's edge should be a straight line because this point is the farthest from you. About $1/2$" from the beginning, move the hoop right to left in a zigzag fashion to sketch the top line of the path. Make the space between the zigzag lines longer the farther to the left you stitch. Repeat for the other side of the path.

㉜ See Thread #26. Repeat Step 31 for the 2nd path color, going over and below the path stitches already in place.

㉝ Distant mountains and hills—Reposition the hoop and follow Steps 15-29 to sketch the remaining distant shrubs, mountains, hills, and river grass. Note that Shrub 12 is sketched with Thread #15.

㉞ Left path—See Threads #25 and 26. Reposition the hoop to encompass the left side of the path. Repeat Steps 31–32 to sketch the upper and lower path lines.

㉟ Foreground squiggles—See Threads #27 and 28. Refer to the master pattern for terrain lines and sketch the squiggly lines underneath the path. Rehoop to sketch the squiggly lines in the right foreground.

WASHING AWAY THE STABILIZER

❶ Cut away the excess front and back stabilizers (do not remove the fusible interfacing). Run water over the fabric using your fingers to help remove the stabilizer. Once the "gooey" stabilizer is gone, work in some soap on the front and back for 2–3 minutes to help remove the stabilizer around the threads. Then soak until the stabilizer is removed. Blot dry and allow to air dry.

❷ When dry, use a pressing cloth to press both sides.

COLORING THE BACKGROUND FABRIC

❶ See figure 6 and page 117 for colored pencil sketching ideas. Using a combination of the 4 green Prismacolor colored pencils, lay each pencil on its side and lightly sketch these colors on the foreground (an example has been dashed on the master pattern), the foreground shrubs, distant shrubs and the hills. Lightly pencil sketch some green around the base of the poppies. Don't get the color too dark and don't let the green infringe on the flower petals.

❷ Use the yellow pencil to color some sections of the sky, making random strokes throughout. See the master pattern for cloud formation ideas. Sketch a sun at the center dip in the mountains. Sketch some yellow highlights on the river and the mountains underneath the sun.

❸ Use the light blue pencil to randomly sketch some blue clouds and the water on the river.

4 Use the light brown pencil to lightly sketch inside the path.

5 Evaluate all the colors and intensify the colors where necessary.
Note: Should you be unhappy with the color results, take a white eraser (test on a sample first) and erase some of the color. Or if you want to get rid of all the color, simply hand wash the fabric with some mild soap. Depending on the fabric you used, most, if not all, of the color will wash out and you can start over.

6 Let the background air dry. Press from the back using a pressing cloth.

THREAD SKETCHING THE CLOUDS AND FOREGROUND

1 Insert a white bobbin. See Thread #29. Outline all the yellow clouds in the hoop, starting and stopping with 5–6 small stitches.

2 See Thread #28. Repeat Step 1 to sketch the blue clouds.

3 Continue moving the hoop to complete all the yellow and blue clouds.

4 Use the pink pencil to lightly sketch some pink sky between the yellow and blue clouds.

FINISHING THE QUILT

1 Square up the quilt. Make sure that the landscape is level and not tilting.

2 Add borders, batting, and backing.

3 Quilt the top, with polyester invis-

ible thread stitching over all the thread-sketched lines except for the river.

4 Block the quilt.

5 Attach the binding and label.

Figure 6
Background with colored pencil sketches.

SETTING THE COLORS

1 Mix 1 tablespoon of either Delta Ceramcoat or Jo Sonja's Textile Medium with a couple of drops of Versatex. (This eliminates having to heat set the final product.)

2 Dip the fabric brush into this mixture and lightly paint on the textile medium mixture.

3 Let air dry.

Tip: *See* Quilts of a Different Color *by Irena Bluhm (AQS, 2008) for more detailed instruction on setting the colored pencils.*

Thread Chart for POPPIES ON PARADE

Thread number		Design	Thread color	Hoop movement
1	Poppy petals	1st color petal	Medium red	Follow outline
2	Poppy center	Flower center Flower anthers	Charcoal	R–L Follow lines
3	Poppy petals	2nd color petal	Cranberry	Follow outline
4		3rd color petal	Medium coral	Same
5	Poppy leaves	1st color stem and leaf	Medium-dark green	Same
6		2nd color stem and leaf	Medium green	Same
7		3rd color stem and leaf	Light green	Same
8	Dirt at river's edge	Dirt	Medium brown	Follow river's edge
9	Foreground shrubs	Shrubs 1 & 5	Medium-dark green	Follow outline
10		Shrubs 2 & 4	Medium green	Same
11		Shrub 3	Medium olive	Same
12	Distant river shrubs	Line under shrubs	Medium-dark green	Follow line
13		Shrubs 6, 8, & 13	Light green	Follow outline
14		Shrubs 7, 9, 10, & 11	Medium light green	Same
15		Shrub 12	Medium olive	Same
16	Distant mountains	Outline mountains River line	Medium-jeans blue	Same Follow river line
17	Mountain squiggles	1st color mountain squiggle	Medium blue	Follow outline
18		2nd color mountain squiggle	Light gray	Same
19	Hills above river	Outline hills	Medium-dark green	Same
20	Hill squiggles	1st color hill squiggle	Medium-light green	Same
21		2nd color hill squiggle	Light green	Same
22	River grass	1st color grass	Light taupe	Follow lines
23		2nd color grass	Medium olive	Same
24		3rd color grass	Medium-light green	Same
25	Path	1st color path	Medium taupe	Follow outline
26		2nd color path	Light taupe	Same
27	Foreground squiggles	1st foreground squiggle	Medium-light green	Follow line
28		2nd foreground squiggle	Light green	Same
29	Clouds	1st color cloud	Canary yellow	Follow lines of clouds
30		2nd color cloud	Light blue	Same

Master pattern for POPPIES ON PARADE. *Enlarge 135%.*

Troubleshooting

Why is the thread looping?

– – – The top tension is too loose. Move the tension dial to a higher number.

– – – You're moving the hoop erratically. Use a controlled, even speed.

– – – The presser bar is up. Since a free-motion foot hovers above the throat plate, it is easy to forget to put the foot down.

– – – You're threading the machine with the presser foot down. Always thread the machine with the presser foot up. The thread must fall between the tension discs located at the top of the thread path. With the presser foot down the tension discs close, making it difficult for the thread to fall between them.

– – – The fabric or stabilizer is too loose in the hoop. Reposition the stabilizer until it is taut in the hoop.

Why is the bobbin thread breaking?

– – – The bobbin tension is too tight. Loosen the bobbin tension.

– – – The bobbin is inserted incorrectly into the bobbin case.

– – – The bobbin case is not clean. A little maintenance goes a long way.

Why does my top thread keep breaking?

– – – The top tension is too tight. Turn the tension toward 0 or minus (not to 0).

– – – The needle may be bent or burred.

– – – You're moving the hoop too quickly. Relax and move the hoop slowly and smoothly.

– – – Thread is caught on the rough edge of the spool, usually the cut in the top or bottom of the spool where the thread is secured. Carefully use an X-Acto knife to cut away the rough edge.

– – – The needle size is too small. Change to a larger needle.

– – – The thread is too old. Buy new thread.

– – – Your pedal speed is inconsistent. Run the machine at an even speed.

– – – The timing on the machine is off. Take it in for service.

Why does the bobbin thread show on top of the thread appliqué?

– – – Thread is caught on the upper spindle.

– – – The bobbin tension is too loose. Adjust the screw by turning it to the right; secure a few practice stitches until the tension is correct. Purchase a second bobbin case to make adjustments if you are not comfortable making changes to the bobbin case calibrated for your machine.

Resources

See Nancy's website **www.nancyprince.com** and click on Nancy's Book to purchase the custom printed background fabric for A Summer Day, Golden Days, First Snowfall, Spring's Morning, and Searching for Butterflies. If you are appliquéing your own background fabric and do not want to make the small houses and barns, they can be purchased online, too.

Available also are all stabilizers, stencil cutter, and 6" wooden machine embroidery hoops.

To download the FREE quilting detail for the 4 circle quilts and Searching for Butterflies, click on the Book menu tab.

Jo-Ann Fabrics
http://www.joann.com/joann/home/home.jsp

Jo Sonja's Textile Medium and Delta Ceramcoat
www.holcraft.com

Michaels
http://www.michaels.com/

Quilts of a Different Color by Irena Bluhm (AQS, 2008)
www.americanquilter.com

Superior Threads
www.superiorthreads.com

Versatex Fixer
www.dharmatrading.com

YLI Threads
www.ylicorp.com or online stores

About the Author

Nancy's introduction to needle and thread came from a very creative mother who introduced her at an early age to a sewing machine. As a result, fabric and a trusty assortment of sewing machines have been a large part of Nancy's life, but it wasn't until about 11 years ago that she literally stumbled into her adventure with thread painting.

Finding herself in totally unchartered territory and with few references to perfect her skills, she drew on her sewing skills and her somewhat primitive artistic skills to begin a wonderful journey. There was a ton of trial and even more error in her first few quilts, but in a short period of time everything came together and she knew she had found her passion.

Nancy has won numerous awards for her quilts and she enjoys sharing ideas, techniques, and more importantly, laughter and fun with her students. Her first book, *Quilt Savvy: Simple Thread Painting*, was published in 2004 by AQS.

In addition to her husband, Tom, she has three grown sons and eight adorable grandchildren—and three talented daughters-in-law. She spends most of her time juggling her family, quilting, and teaching. This passion for thread painting has enriched her life and keeps her centered and focused.

Please visit Nancy's website at www.nancyprince.com to see more of her work, the free and for-pay videos, information on her workshops and teaching schedule, and to find out a bit more about her work. Don't hesitate to contact her via emailnancy@nancyprince.com if you have any thread-painting questions.

Have fun thread painting!!

other AQS Books

This is only a small selection of the books available from the American Quilter's Society. AQS books are known worldwide for timely topics, clear writing, beautiful color photos, and accurate illustrations and patterns. The following books are available from your local bookseller, quilt shop, or public library.

#8351

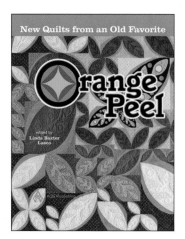

#8350

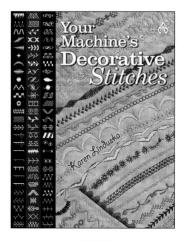

#8353

#8349

#8347

#8146

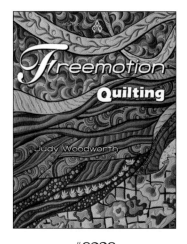

#8238

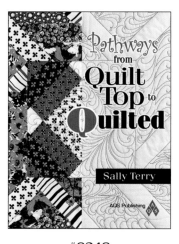

#8348

#8235